MINDSET

Mastery

AWARENESS, MEDITATION, MINDFULNESS, AND MANIFESTATION FOR THE SPIRITUAL WARRIOR

LAURA DI FRANCO

Featuring: Colleen Avis, Eddie BenAbraham, Frank Byrum, Patrick Fisher, Anuka Gazara, Carrie Hopkins-Doubts, Sharon Josef, Amber Kleid, Justin Krull, Rika Rivka Markel, Tiffany McBride, Lori Pieper, Dr. Christy Robinson, Seth Rohrer, Natasha Sharma, Jeanne Lauren Smith, Jennifer Sproul, Star Studenivic, Dr. Amy Wisner

MINDSET
Mastery

Awareness, Meditation,
Mindfulness, and Manifestation
for the Spiritual Warrior

LAURA DI FRANCO

Featuring: Colleen Avis, Eddie BenAbraham, Frank Byrum, Patrick Fisher,
Anuka Gazara, Carrie Hopkins-Doubts, Sharon Josef, Amber Kleid,
Justin Krull, Rika Rivka Markel, Tiffany McBride, Lori Pieper,
Dr. Christy Robinson, Seth Rohrer, Natasha Sharma,
Jeanne Lauren Smith, Jennifer Sproul, Star Studonivic, Dr. Amy Wisner

Free writing and business resources for Brave Healers can be found at: https://lauradifranco.com/resources-vault/

DEDICATION

For all our teachers—the ones we chose, and the ones who showed up whether we wanted them to or not—thank you for guiding us to understanding what's possible.

DISCLAIMER

This book offers health and nutritional information and is designed for educational purposes only. You should not rely on this information as a substitute for, nor does it replace professional medical advice, diagnosis, or treatment. If you have any concerns or questions about your mental, physical, or emotional health, you should always consult with a physician or other healthcare professional. Do not disregard, avoid, or delay obtaining medical or health-related advice from your healthcare professional because of something you may have read here. The use of any information provided in this book is solely at your own risk.

Developments in medical research may impact the health, fitness, and nutritional advice that appears here. No assurances can be given that the information contained in this book will always include the most relevant findings or developments with respect to the particular material.

Having said all that, know that the experts here have shared their tools, practices, and knowledge with you with a sincere and generous intent to assist you on your health and wellness journey. Please contact them with any questions you may have about the techniques or information they provided. They will be happy to assist you further!

TABLE OF CONTENTS

LETTER TO READERS ABOUT THE HEALING CRISIS

The healing crisis is a phenomenon that occurs on the healing journey. It's a form of awareness that is great to understand as you dive into these chapters. A healing crisis occurs when we feel the energy of an old wound, injury, or trauma as it's coming up to be released or healed. The resistance comes up in the form of thoughts, sensations, feelings, emotions, memories, and sometimes pain. Many times these experiences feel exactly like those you felt when the insult occurred.

Notice your reactions to them.

Sometimes it's exactly what you're having the most resistance around (words, ideas, practices, conversations, events, etc.) that are the biggest opportunity for healing. Skilled healers recognize this, and assist their clients through it with tools such as dialoguing, energy work, hands-on practices or modalities, and mindset or awareness coaching, among others.

The healing crisis, and your own resistance, are each an opportunity to go a layer deeper. They are doors to release and relief—to healing.

The problem, sometimes, is that when one is in the middle of a healing crisis, it feels like you're going to die (meaning) the sensations, feelings, and emotions that surface can be that intense. The healers in this book get it. And we're here for you.

If you purchased this book (or it was gifted to you) you have access to a very special private Facebook group where our author experts are hanging out to assist readers with questions, support, or to take the conversation further. This is an incredible benefit to owning this book. You're not alone. We're here to help you. Your questions will be welcomed and your concerns honored. You'll enjoy a safe space to continue your work of healing, and a community that has your back.

Find us in The Brave Healer Book Club.

See you there!

INTRODUCTION

Are you a mindset geek like me? I couldn't wait to publish this book! Awareness and mindset are *everything* when it comes to living your gorgeous, juicy, beautiful life, no matter what circumstances you might be in currently. I have the total honor and pleasure of presenting you with a book full of teachers, coaches, and health and wellness professionals who not only agree with that statement but are about to lay down their master teachings for you on the subject.

Before we start, you know you never truly master anything, right? This is a journey. The destination of mastery doesn't really exist. You arrived here today with a particular definition and set of beliefs taught to you by someone (a teacher, parent, coach, friend, mentor, boss, etc.), and it's driving your thoughts, beliefs, and behaviors—essentially creating your life.

What if there's something you haven't learned yet that could change everything?

Mastery is a life-long practice. Mastering your mindset means you understand that. If you're like me, you have a beginner's or learner's mindset. This was one of the principles we learned in my marital arts training. As soon as we earned our black belts, we knew what we didn't know, not what we knew. It was about the next level of training. The mastery was the moment-to-moment mindset, and how we were able to respond in that moment to what was presented to us.

Get ready for the ride that is your mind and all the ways to discover, know, heal, retrain, and optimize it. Get ready to read stories that might blow that mind, with perspectives that immediately immerse you in the high vibe energy of gratitude. Get ready to learn things that change everything about what you thought was possible.

"I want to tell them what an incredible gift they're about to receive." I was a motormouth that day to my healer friend who was listening to me go on about this book idea. "God, I love this topic! I can't believe I didn't think of this sooner! This is going to change people's lives!"

Brave Healer books are a living energy, each a part of a larger mission and community that has grown over the last several years. You're about to dive into chapters from people who raised their hands when the Universe asked, "Are you ready to walk your walk?" You're about to learn life-changing tools, practices, and strategies culminating in lifetimes' worth of training and discipline. Each brave word laid down on these pages is a gift of awareness. Will you take a deep, pelvic bowl breath now and join us for a most powerful experience of knowing yourself at a deeper level? Will you ask yourself, "What else is possible?" when life knocks you down again? Will you take on the challenge to get still and listen to the messages of your mind-body-soul, guiding you to your best possible life?

These things are just a taste of what you're about to experience here with our experts.

We usually practice "setting our mind" in an attempt toward success or happiness, whatever definitions we use. Souls choosing to practice mindset, awareness, mindfulness, meditation, manifestation, or other forms of observation and inquiry, are warriors. You're on a quest toward a better, healthier, more aligned, exciting, and joyful life. We were born for these things!

Something in you knows that. It's the warrior who fights for it rather than becoming resigned to a mediocre existence. The warrior hears the call in their heart to go after the joy and then takes the first step, trusting they'll be guided. The warrior chooses to rest rather than give up the fight. With awareness, the warrior gets a choice, and that warrior always chooses love over fear.

Here in this book, you'll be surrounded by fellow spiritual warriors. If you've been feeling alone, you can't use that as an excuse anymore. You now have a heart-centered team of experts, healers, coaches, and good people to journey with. What you hold in your hands isn't just a book; it's access to a powerful community. Welcome. We're so glad you're here!

On my journey, mastering my mindset has been about overcoming fear and self-sabotage. I spent so much of my life working on this that I wrote a couple of whole books about it. It's what keeps people small and sometimes paralyzed. The most important thing I learned about mindset is that my body is the door to the practice. I changed the word mindful to 'bodyful.' I recognized that grounding, centering, and in general, being in my body was the first and most powerful part of the practice and the only way I could begin to notice, listen to, and hear the powerful messages being given to me every day. The body is the gateway to your inner wisdom, healer, and power.

I invite you to drop into the sacred space of your body now as you begin this journey with us. Clear your mind and connect with your breath. Feel the air move in and out, and the torso and ribs expand and contract. Notice the sound of your heartbeat and the taste in your mouth. Focus on the energy within you. In this place, you'll find the answers to everything you're aching to know. It's this inner place, this attention to what you notice, where you'll have the opportunity to manifest every deep desire. In this inner place of focus, you'll receive messages from your higher self, inspiration for your life, and answers to what is aligned with your soul's calling.

Practice being here as you read. Allow reading this book to be a practice of staying here in this moment and noticing everything.

You know that fear of not-good-enough keeping you from living the life you were born for? It's boring. Make a date with your mistakes and failures and recognize each as a stepping stone.

How's Next Tuesday?
By Laura Di Franco

There was a knock at the door
and I knew
so I peeked through the hole first.
I shouldn't have opened the door
but I did.
Failure and her sister Mistake
wanted to have lunch.
"Sorry, I'm busy writing poetry," I said.

They persisted.
I resisted.
They convinced.
I winced.
They went on and on.
I recognized that boring song
and I closed the door in their face.

Another knock came.
And muffled words from outside the door,
"We're not what you think we are,"
they pleaded.
But the fear of what others would think
if they saw me having lunch with the enemy
sunk in, and I said,
"Go away; I don't want to play today."

The following week my phone rang.
A familiar number showed
so I pressed green.
"Hello?"
Failure was back on the line and this time
it was clear; she had an agenda.
Fear flushed through my gut
to my cheeks
but before I could hang up
she eeeked out the words,
"I swear I'm your friend."

I was curious.
"What do you mean?"
"You always seem to make me feel bad,"
I said.
"You always make me feel stupid and sad."
She sighed.
"That's you feeling that way," she replied.
"That's you thinking I'm something to avoid."
"That's you making your heartache mean more than it should."

I was confused.
"What do you mean?" I asked again.
"Every time you visit
I'm reminded I'm not enough."
"I'm sure others will see you and steer clear."

"Nobody wants to be seen with failure!" I shouted,
sure I offended her, but not caring.
Failure was amused.
"What if you needed me?" she said.
"What if you'd never succeed without me?" She teased.

Now I was mad.
"What the fuck do you mean by that?"
"Relax, take a breath," she said.
"If you never get to know me,
if you never learn to dance with me like that,
if you never take risks and fall,
or start the journey toward your dreams,
by seeing me repeatedly,
you'll never understand,
you'll never succeed.
Because it's failure you need
to get anywhere worth going."

I stared at the phone
took another deep breath
and realized
I'd been hiding all my life
from the one thing
sure to get me to the place
I've always longed to be.
And the more she showed her face
the more I hid,
not realizing I should have been
excited instead.
Because one more date with failure
meant one more step toward my dream.

"So how's next Tuesday?" I said.

When you're faced with your fears, again, you may have a moment where you look up to the sky and say, "Haven't I already dealt with this?"

There's always another layer, isn't there, brave healers? Sorry to tell you, my dear mindset masters, this is part of what we signed up for. A lifelong healing journey means there's no destination of perfection or mastery. It means we chose to be teachers, and we're doing the work until we die. Then, maybe, we will do it again in the next life.

By the way, I'm convinced I had at least one past life as a cowgirl and another as a race car driver. Either that or my ancestors passed down some pretty crazy I-feel-the-need-for-speed genes. Anyone else used to love *Speed Racer* Saturday morning cartoons?

Whatever the challenge presented to me, I accept.

Whether I think I've dealt with it already, the Universe has other plans, or she's testing me so I can level up, I accept.

With a team of spiritual warriors by my side, I accept.

I'm not alone. I'm not giving up. I'm here with absolute faith in what I was born for. And I accept the challenge.

Whatever is thrown my way moving forward, I accept the challenge to show up, speak up, and to love as hard and as much as possible. That includes loving myself—completely and radically.

This girl is a love warrior. She's here to change the world. And so are each of the authors in this book. We're ready to help you practice the awareness, transform the pain, discover your purpose, and guide you to the life you dream about. You're in capable, brave, skilled, and loving hands. Grab hold, and let's walk together.

As you receive the gifts each of our authors has to give, keep a notebook and pen nearby. Write down your a-has, questions, or moments of healing or transformation. Save the quotes you love. Email the authors (they have offered their contact information) and let them know how their brave words affected you. They are generously there for you to answer your questions, offer support, and help you with the next steps on your journey.

This is more than a book; it's a powerful toolkit and community. Thank you for being part of it!

With Warrior Love,

Laura

Chapter 1

MINDSET MASTERY MAGIC

HOW TO CREATE THE LIFE OF YOUR DREAMS

Laura Di Franco, MPT, Publisher

MY STORY

My official mindset journey kicked off when Oprah did the book club program with Eckhart Tolle for *A New Earth*. I couldn't get enough of that conversation. I showed up on time every week, knowing another moment of transformation was in store.

That book was published in 2008, the same year I opened my first business, Bodyworks Physical Therapy. Love you, crazy Universe!

That was also the year I began writing for others to read with my blog. Four years after that (after six years of training in Taekwondo with my son and earning our black belts together), I published my first book, *Living, Healing, and Taekwondo*. I had a few things to say. I was just only beginning to find and use my voice.

I thought I knew a lot about healing and life, but I didn't know what I didn't know. Life threw me more tests. The nine-hour black belt exam paled in comparison to what I faced in years after that. I'm so glad Master

H. made us earn that belt. I'm so glad I knew what I was made of before embarking on the rest of the journey. I'm so glad I got up every time life knocked me down. And I'm so glad that after hitting the wall, I still got up and carried on.

In Taekwondo, we follow five tenets:

Courtesy
Integrity
Perseverance
Self-control
Indomitable spirit

The indomitable spirit, and persevering in holding onto it, served me the most in my practice.

The practice (and now my discipline) of awareness, starting with how Tolle taught us to observe our thoughts, and including my decades of training with masters in somato-emotional bodywork, martial arts, and healing modalities, was the way I survived the biggest tests. It's also the way I thrive and manifest my dream life, even during the worst possible moments.

If you look up the top five most stressful life events, you'll find:

Death of a loved one
Divorce
Moving
Major illness or injury
Job loss

How many of those have you experienced? If you've lived long enough, probably all of them. I've experienced all of these. One of the keys to mastering your mindset—which allows you to thrive despite life's biggest challenges—is detachment. The Brave Healer version of detaching from the outcome is what I want to share here.

"Whether you're elated or severely depressed, the challenge is not to attach. You can't always attach to the elated feeling as a goal. Life brings both. Don't make either mean anything." Wise words from my acupuncturist.

My teachers, including my Taekwondo master, acupuncturist, myofascial release therapists, breath-worker, Reiki healer, psychotherapist, hypnotist, and ex-husband, have all taught me one main thing: I'm worthy because I was born. This was the foundation of my lifelong healing journey.

And when things are "bad," it's the worthiness up on the surface, again, no matter how many times I may have been there.

In their various ways, words, lack of words, nudges, treatment, actions, etc., my teachers gave me a wake-up call to pay attention to what I made things mean in my head: *You're not worthy.* I began noticing what my thoughts were, based on the moment presented to me. I began to reclaim my worth.

With awareness, we have a choice. And those six words may just be the most powerful in all of the universe.

Up until waking up and paying attention, life seemed out of my control, happening *to* me—a bunch of disappointments or victories. So, of course, I always wanted more of the good stuff and made those victories, wins, or achievements the goal. Life was good as long as good things were happening. That meant that my happiness was conditional and not in my control. I was so good at achieving things: Straight As, degrees (two of them), a great job, a promotion, getting married, having kids, running a marathon (or three), earning my black belt, opening my first business, or my second. But when achievements are the only way you feel good, what happens when things fail? When achievement is how you define your worth, what happens when you make a big mistake or fail?

The thing is, happiness is (and was always) up to me, no matter what I achieved or didn't. And detaching from the outcome is the main key to being happy no matter what is happening to you. You were born, so you're worthy.

Stop making your worth about everyone else's idea of success. I started to taste joy when I began changing my thoughts and behaviors to align with what I wanted instead of what everyone else told me I should want.

Everything happens *for* you.

When you realize everything happens *for* you, not *to* you, it's a little easier to detach. A seemingly bad event could lead to consequences later on that are quite favorable. The problem is that you can't see the good stuff when the bad event is happening. Your reactions take over, including attaching to a "good" outcome. All of a sudden, life sucks. You're blind to the bigger picture.

"You're being demoted from your manager position, and we're moving half your hours to another location."

The blow to my ego was almost too much to bear. Detaching from this outcome of being demoted would take years. Looking back, it was absolutely a favor the Universe did for me. I couldn't see it then and cried for weeks, finally quitting that job because of the verbal abuse my new manager was dishing out to me and the other employees. I ended up partnering with a new company and opening up three new physical therapy locations. This was a hugely positive move for my career.

What if we trusted the bigger picture all the time?

"Rejection is protection." One of my mentors says this in our mastermind session, and I think about detaching from the outcome. "Something better is in store. Don't attach to the outcome or how the Universe is organizing things in your favor or possibly protecting you." I get this. I practice trusting as I hear her talk.

Detach from the outcome.

Then, of course, life will throw you another test, just to see what you're made of, to see if you really mean what you say and are willing to walk your walk of brave healing no matter what.

Breathe, Laura. Do your box breathing.

Inhale. . . one, two, three, four. Hold. . . one, two, three, four. Exhale. . . one, two, three, four. Hold. . . one, two, three, four. I repeated it five times.

Is that better? I don't know. OMG, they're going to find me passed out on the floor in here. My chest hurts.

I paced in a small room just outside the courtroom doors—a holding room for witnesses. I was alone. It was 12 feet by 12 feet with a short grey carpet and a small wooden table with four matching chairs. Each witness was sequestered before (and after) their testimony, so they didn't talk to others about it.

I'm going to die in here.

Maybe the feeling was due to the unknown. This was my Saber-Toothed tiger. The feelings consumed me. My mind blared, choking me with nonsense and constant repetitive thoughts, trying to sort out the minutes that lay before me in any sensible way. There was no sorting this out ahead of time, though.

I turned toward one of the wooden chairs and started doing push-ups on the back edge. "When you're really nervous before a talk, it helps to get physical," I remember a speaking coach saying. "Do some jumping jacks, or knee bends, or push-ups."

Is that better? Maybe a tiny bit. I don't know. OMG.

I closed my eyes and listened to the beat of my heart. I felt nauseous. There was a knock at the door, and an officer peeked in: "Ready for you."

He escorted me into the courtroom and through the swinging doors that separated the front of the room (judge, jury, attorney's tables) from the back (spectators). The officer pointed to the witness chair and motioned to the opening at the side where I could step into the wooden box and take my seat.

OMG, this looks like a coffin.

Through most of my experiences in court, I was significantly attached to "winning." When this case ended in a mistrial, I heard, "Rejection is protection." It took several days to come off of the adrenaline rush of fear, what ifs, and the mind-fuck. I didn't snap back quickly. I watched myself dwell in the dark alley of my mind for days. I wasn't fun to be around. But I did have tools and powerful friends.

"You really don't know how this is playing out. What if this is what needs to happen for the bigger picture to unfold in exactly the way it needs to for everyone's highest purpose and good?"

Honestly, I heard those words from a coach, and the Devil may have whispered, *fuck everyone's highest good; we need a win.*

I'm a work in progress. But I came around. I fell back into my practice, my discipline of trust, surrender, acceptance, awareness, and deep breaths. Despite experiencing some of the worst anxiety, worry, and fear in my life, I came out on the other side of my experience feeling stronger and way more aligned.

I didn't get there alone like I tried to do so many times in the past. This time, I reached out to people. I moved through the story right away. People (skilled people) listened to me. They called me out on my bullshit. "Laura, I get it; this sucks. But your energy is swirling. Let's get you out of the swirl." Thanks, John.

I woke up again. I remembered. I allowed myself to feel what was there and then chose something more aligned, healthy, helpful, and aimed at what I desired for my life. I had to shake myself back awake sometimes.

Everyone needs a nudge to remember their practice when the fire gets hot. When life throws you something that challenges your ability to detach, it's about waking up in that moment as quickly as possible (with the help of friends if needed) and getting back on your track and in your body. These moves are ninja moves. They're a result of the ongoing practice and mastery of awareness. I consider it "mastery" when I can choose this in seconds. That feels badass to me.

There are so many layers and levels to move through. Understanding the triggers and getting to know myself more deeply has been a game-changer. Watching my thoughts, like watching a movie, as a spectator, offered me a space to detach. I often thought, *hmm, that's interesting; I wonder what else is possible?*

The pause was the most powerful of my ninja moves. The pause and the breath give me space to maneuver when the chaos of my habitual mind takes over. The pause helps me remember I have a choice. The pause, a breath, dropping my awareness down into my belly, and asking myself a powerful question changed my life and helped me become a master of my own mind.

Mastering my mind helped me create a life I love, a successful, purposeful, world-changing business, relationships that grow and evolve into bigger love, and the daily excitement of knowing I can make anything happen—ninja moves.

My inner ninja teacher: *Wake up and remember you have a choice right now. Do you want to stay in this hurt, pain, resentment, or anger? Or do you want to move back to something more high vibe?*

Me: *Well, duh, I want love.*

My inner ninja teacher: *Well, then, what are you waiting for?*

THE PRACTICE

THE NINJA'S GUIDE TO CREATING A LIFE-CHANGING MINDSET DISCIPLINE

Practicing ninja-level mindset moves requires a few simple things:

1. Being able to feel (notice thoughts, feelings, emotions, sensations).
2. Pausing when triggered and moving back into the body.
3. Taking action toward a higher vibe and more aligned thought, belief, or behavior as fast as possible.

1. **Practice feeling**

   Grab a notebook and pen, and let's start your journey with something simple. Find a comfortable space without distractions and practice three to five minutes of meditation or breathwork, in any form you enjoy. Get still, clear your mind, and practice grounding and centering into your body. Being in your body is the way you develop a ninja-level mindset discipline. Do a few minutes of this before moving on to the writing.

   When you're ready, set a timer for five minutes and start to write by filling in the blank: I feel _____. Write as fast as you can without censoring yourself. Explore all the ways you can feel while you write: physical sensations (including what you see, hear, taste, smell, and feel), and mental or emotional thoughts or feelings. Include anything coming up for you without attaching to what that is. Keep breathing and centering as you write. You can practice this body awareness-writing combo daily. It's a powerful practice that will help you connect to your inner wisdom.

2. **Notice a trigger and pause**

   Pausing yourself during a triggering moment is challenging. That's why these are ninja moves! You can practice awareness around this in a couple of ways. First, take a moment to journal about the things that most annoy, anger, or irritate you. What has come up in the recent past when you noticed you were spun up or reacting before you could help it? Journal about the feelings, thoughts, and circumstances, especially noting the list of inner thoughts about these scenarios. You're using journaling to shed light on these things. It's an awareness tool. Get to know your own triggers well. Notice everything. Be curious. What do you feel in your body when this happens? Do you notice your body at all? Describe the body sensations attached to the triggers.

Next, you'll have to practice waking up in the middle of a trigger and pausing your reaction. This takes practice. The next time you're irritated, annoyed, hurt, angry, or otherwise about to blow, pause with a few deep breaths and begin an inquiry before you say or do anything. Can you get to ten deep breaths without reacting? Can you sleep on it? Can you talk to a trusted friend before you react? Take out your journal and write out every detail of the trigger, especially the thoughts and feelings you're having. Don't censor yourself. Notice what happens when you pause and take these actions.

Side note: The healthy release of anger or frustration is incredibly important. My friend and coach, Jen Piceno, calls this 'sacred rage.' The idea is not to stuff it; it's to feel and release it. Writing can be a very therapeutic way to do that. So can punching a pillow or screaming at the top of your lungs with loud music in your car. Yeah, I've done all of those things. The key to this practice is truly the awareness moments, which give you a choice and opportunity to align to something more high vibe.

3. **Choose love**

   Your practice has included feeling, and you're getting better at noticing everything you think and feel. Great job. You've even trained yourself to pause during a triggering moment of anger or hurt. You're practicing ninja moves, baby; great job!

   Now, the choice is yours. When you have enough awareness to feel and pause, you have the ability to choose your next step, the action that'll most quickly align with the highest vibration there is—love.

   What would love do?

   What would love say?

   How would love sort this out?

   It can feel very vulnerable to show up in the world with love as your weapon, which, by the way, is the ultimate ninja move of awareness (vulnerability). When you practice this way, making love your discipline, you infuse every cell of your body with that energy. Miracles happen when you choose love.

Make sure to take out your journal in these moments and write down your A-ha moments, moments of healing and transformation, and stories of love. Share those brave words with the world. The key to this practice is noticing, choosing, and moving toward love more quickly each time. As you master the practice, you'll notice almost instant shifts. This is the magic.

A final note about manifesting the life of your dreams. Your awareness practice and your love discipline (or lack of it) create your life in every moment. Typically what we all want is a feeling. We go for the achievements, obtain the objects, attempt the relationships, all because we think that having those things will give us the feeling we're after. I love love. I love the feeling of gratitude. I love ease and joy. I love feeling these ways.

I noticed I achieved those elated feelings after the good stuff in my life happened, but afterward, when the event was over, the object obtained, or the achievement completed, I looked for the next high. That became exhausting. I learned, instead, how to feel great any time. I learned how to access the vibration of love and gratitude, or ease and joy, whenever I want to. I make joy the pursuit - tiny moments of focus on something in front of me right now - not something I don't have. And all of a sudden, those feelings become the norm. I don't have to reach for an achievement to access them.

For my law of attraction fans who understand the science of good vibes, you know what that means: I keep attracting love, gratitude, joy, and ease.

Every single second of every single day, I get to choose. It's only a matter of waking up to what's possible in the moment, pausing if I'm feeling something not-so-good, and gently moving in a different direction.

When life allows me to heal a deeper wound, I wake up to that, too, giving myself full permission to feel the pain but not allowing myself to get stuck there. Energy is meant to move. And I have control over that movement. I get to flip the switch when I'm ready.

I wanted to write a mindset book because of what creating the discipline of awareness did for me. This practice, and every one of the expert tools you'll learn in this book, will be the key to pretty much anything you desire in life. It's kinda cool to have that kind of toolkit.

Now, I challenge you to go practice. It's in the moments of practice that the magic will occur. What do you feel right now? What miracle do you notice right this moment? Take a big, juicy, full pelvic bowl breath. If you were successful, you have something magnificent to be grateful for—living.

My wish for you is to live each moment fiercely alive, in love, joy, and gratitude, knowing you were born, so you're worthy, and that the life you dream of is already right here.

Laura Di Franco, MPT, is the CEO of Brave Healer Productions, where they specialize in publishing and business strategy for healers. She spent 30 years in holistic physical therapy and 12 of those in private practice before making the pivot to publishing. With 14 years of training in the martial arts and 50 books and counting, including over three dozen Amazon bestsellers, she knows how to help you share your brave words in a way that builds your business and your dream life.

Her daily mission is to help fellow wellness practitioners do what they need to do to change the world in less time and with fewer mistakes and heartache on the journey. She shares her authentic journey, wisdom, and expertise with refreshing transparency and straightforward badassery. Hold on to your seat because riding alongside her means you'll be pushed into and beyond your comfort zone and having way more fun with your purpose-driven fears on a regular basis.

When Laura chills out, you'll find her with a mojito at a poetry event with friends, driving her Mustang, bouncing to the beat at a rave, or on a beach in Mexico with something made of dark chocolate in her mouth.

Connect with Laura:

https://LauraDiFranco.com

https://www.Facebook.com/BraveHealerbyLaura/

https://www.Instagram.com/BraveHealerProductions

https://www.Twitter.com/Brave_Healer

https://www.linkedin.com/in/laura-di-franco-mpt-1b037a5/

https://www.youtube.com/@bravehealerproductions2444

"Taking responsibility for everything (every thought) in your life means total freedom. With awareness you get a choice. What thoughts, beliefs, and actions are you choosing today?"

~ Laura Di Franco

Chapter 2

HEALING GRIEF THROUGH SELF-COMPASSION

MEETING LOSS WITH A GROWTH MINDSET

Carrie Hopkins-Doubts, MA, PCC

MY STORY

"What are the gifts your grief has given you?" I absolutely hate that question.

It's a valuable one, but one you have to be ready for.

A stranger asked me that question two weeks after my husband died. *I can't think of a single gift right now, and fuck-you for asking,* I thought. I stared blankly at him, unable to speak. I wanted to kick him and run away. Clearly, I was not ready for that question then.

Then, he droned on about the gifts he discovered when his grandmother died, and what I should do to find them. After finally noticing I'd disappeared from the conversation, he asked, "Does this help?"

"No," I said. Then *he* burst into tears. I hugged him. "This is what helps," I said gently to him.

Why am I telling you this story? If you have experienced the loss of someone or something important, you've probably experienced this kind of interaction with a well-meaning person. I'm here to tell you that it's okay to want to protect yourself from people mashing your toes in their hurry to "fix" you so they can feel more comfortable around you.

People assumed that, because I'm a grief coach, I'd have an answer to that question right away. It's been almost a year and a half since Tom's fatal heart attack, and I'm at the point where I have some answers now.

The greatest gift of my grief was that it opened me to a greater capacity for self-compassion as well as compassion for others.

It was the practice I'll share with you at the end of my chapter that was my vehicle for the transformation I ultimately experienced.

First, it's helpful for you to understand what grief is and what it can do to you.

SOME POSSIBLE EXPERIENCES OF GRIEF

Dealing with loss creates stress on all levels: physical, mental, emotional, social, and spiritual. You may be experiencing some or all of the challenges listed below. As you are reading through this section, circle those that apply to you now.

Physical – trouble sleeping, low energy, muscle aches and pains, immune suppression, weight gain/loss, heart palpitations.

Mental – initial denial, disorganized thinking, difficulty concentrating, irrational thoughts, regrets ("shoulda, woulda, coulda"), the judgment of self and others.

Emotional – initial shock and numbness, emotional flooding, sadness, anger, anxiety/fearfulness, guilt, sense of helplessness and hopelessness, longing or yearning for the past.

Social – isolation and withdrawal, avoiding crowds/gatherings, being "dropped" by friends or family, lack of understanding or support from others, difficulties with holidays/anniversaries, loneliness.

Spiritual – a crisis of faith, feeling of abandonment, anger at God, deep questioning *"Why?"*, loss of meaning/purpose, feeling punished or unworthy of love.

There are external, internal, and spiritual adjustments that need to be made as a part of the grieving process to help you to move forward in creating your life's next chapter:

1. **External adjustments** – Life changes dramatically when a person or thing (i.e., a job) that has been an integral part of your life is no longer there. You may need to go out and get a new job, change careers, sell your home, move to another city, learn new skills, become a single parent, and so on. Life changes like these can seem overwhelming, especially when they come all at once.

2. **Internal adjustments** – Creating a new identity out of your loss is a challenge when you've counted on a role to define who you are and your value in the world. It can also be transformative and deeply healing. The question, *"Who am I now?"* really comes to the forefront and invites you to find your answer.

3. **Spiritual adjustments** – Profound loss can deeply shake your faith in God/the Universe, leaving you feeling vulnerable and abandoned. It often brings forward the deep question, *"Why am I here, and, what is my purpose?"*

In my personal grief journey, the internal adjustment of no longer being a wife was so difficult. Being a "me" again after being a "we" for so long took a long time to get used to. I felt a dagger in my heart every time I used the wrong pronoun.

What I know to be true: I know that I'm going through an experience of loss and grief, and that's not who I am. That's not "me." Same for you. Grief is not who you are.

POST-TRAUMATIC GROWTH AND THE GROWTH MINDSET

Post-traumatic growth (PTG) is a theory that explains the potential for the positive transformation a person can experience following a trauma. It was developed by psychologists Richard Tedeschi and Lawrence Calhoun in the mid-1990s. The theory is that people who endure psychological struggle following adversity often experience growth, leading to many benefits on the other side of it.

Tedeschi says, "People develop new understandings of themselves, the world they live in, how to relate to other people, the kind of future they might have, and a better understanding of how to live life."

Are certain types of people more prone to experiencing PTG than others? This is an area of ongoing research. My interest is in this question—

what are the conditions under which PTG is more likely to occur in a person who has undergone trauma, loss, and grief?

Carol S. Dweck, the author of *Mindset: The New Psychology of Success*, talks about the distinction between a fixed mindset and a growth mindset.

A fixed mindset creates self-defeating thoughts like, *"I am just not a strong person,"* or *"I'm not smart enough to handle _____."* When we're in a fixed mindset, the natural conclusion is that there's no point in trying to change.

On the other hand, a person with a growth mindset will see a new challenge as an opportunity to learn and grow. Someone with this mindset might think, "I can learn to do this. Who can I ask for help? Are there any other resources that might help?"

I thought about that man's question long after the incident passed. It wasn't a bad question, but it was bad timing. When my emotions were raw and I was in tremendous pain, I couldn't move beyond my feelings into a future space where I could look back, having survived them, and recognize the gifts. I accepted where I was in the healing process, which was not very far at that point. I made it okay.

My thoughts turned to another question to ask myself. Instead of asking the question, "What are the gifts my grief has given me," I started asking myself, "What can I learn from this challenge? What does grief want to teach me?"

These questions open the mind to curiosity, which is the first step in adopting a growth mindset.

As I worked with this question every day, I noticed that I started to learn to be patient and kind towards myself during the times I was struggling. I learned new skills out of necessity. I learned about finances and the legal steps I needed to take, not only to ensure my survival but to leave my affairs in good order for my family when it's time for me to leave the planet. I gained the skill and confidence to handle things on my own that I had depended upon my husband to take care of.

As I leaned and stretched into each new lesson, I learned to trust myself and surrender to the unknown when I felt unsure about my capabilities and what the future holds. Most of all, I learned how to be compassionate with myself and give myself time, space, and generous helpings of loving to heal.

Are you wondering how this works? Here are a few ideas to consider:

- Acknowledge your situation and all the complexities involved.
- Appreciate the ways you are managing/coping with your loss, now.
- Accept the reality of your situation and all your feelings about it.
- Be curious about what your grief is helping you to learn about yourself, your situation, and your life.
- Be patient with yourself while you are learning new skills. No judgments!
- Reflect on and celebrate what you are regularly learning.
- Don't give up, even when it's hard.

So far, these are ideas to consider. How do you put them into practice so they can be integrated into a new belief system that will support you in successfully navigating through your grief journey?

THE POWER OF WRITING

Research shows that writing down your thoughts and feelings contributes to emotional health and healing and even accelerates the process. There are many kinds of writing—creative writing, keeping a diary, journaling, etc. You don't have to be a writer to benefit from daily writing practices.

The practice I'm sharing with you below is a specific kind of writing designed to help you feel, express, and release the difficult emotions of sadness, anger, regret, guilt, fear, etc. It's a safe space for you to process these feelings so that they are not coming up for expression at times and in ways that are destructive or inappropriate—think road rage.

Feelings are the emotional energy that our thoughts ride on. If we have a thought, we have a feeling to match it. If we keep that energy bottled up, it is harmful. It will come out in an exaggerated form, or it can go into our tissue cells and become an illness or disease.

This practice is adapted from the work of Drs. Ron and Mary Hulnick, from the University of Santa Monica.

THE PRACTICE

EMOTIONAL RELEASE WRITING

Putting your thoughts and feelings on paper is an important healing tool as it leads to a therapeutic release of the emotional energy that can be a block to moving forward. I encourage clients who are grieving to engage in a type of journaling I call Emotional Release Writing.

Doing this Emotional Release Writing does two things for you. First, you are giving yourself a safe space to express yourself. Also, you're sending yourself the message, "I'm here for myself."

This practice is a way of setting up a safe space for you to access your feelings, give them a name, express, and release them, in service to freeing up the energy that is stuck there.

The process is simple and meant to be cathartic. First, find a place where you can close the door and not be disturbed. You need total privacy. Put a sign on the door. Tell people in your household what's going on so they don't get alarmed and think you need help.

Get a pad of paper and a pen. Do the process longhand, not on the computer. The physical act of writing—the flow of thoughts from your head down through your hand and onto paper—contributes to the releasing process.

Set your timer for 15 minutes. Write about what comes to mind, writing as fast as possible. There is nothing off-limits here. You can say anything you need to say. You don't need to write in complete sentences, just keep the pen moving to match the speed of your thoughts. Write continuously and don't stop until the timer beeps. (Note: If you find you want to continue after the timer has sounded, just keep going.)

As you are writing, emotions will surface. Keep writing. If it's anger, keep scribbling while you are fuming. If it's sadness, keep writing through your tears.

When the emotional energy is released, you'll know. You'll have a sense of release, lightness, or relief. Sometimes, when the emotional energy has been released you may notice the writing change. When you've surrendered the hurt, anger, and upset to the page, there is often an opening through which your soul can speak words of comfort, encouragement, and faith to you. When you write from the voice of your soul, you often have the experience of telling yourself something incredibly significant that you didn't know you knew.

You'll probably be in a tender place when you stop writing. I recommend spending some quiet time with yourself to flood yourself with loving, do forgiveness work, affirmation work, meditation, or any practice that is gentle and kind towards yourself.

When you are done with the process, take the pages and either shred them immediately or burn them. This is important. Don't read them. Don't leave them around for someone else to find/read.

If you are grieving or experiencing emotional imbalance, I encourage you to do this process at least once a week and spend as much time as you need.

Emotional Release Writing bypasses the logical left-brained way of coping and creates a sense of wholeness, of oneness with it all. It's a multidimensional experience of expressing your hurt and comforting yourself simultaneously.

You can tell yourself where to look for hope when you write. This includes those times when you think you can't take another step. Somehow, when you write your feelings down, the picture starts to emerge where you see yourself taking that step. You see falling and getting up and being held—all as part of life.

Emotional Release Writing is the practice that saved me. It helped anchor me in a growth mindset while meeting myself with patience, compassion, and love every step on my journey through grief.

I encourage you to try it at least a few times. There is no wrong way to do this practice. If you are thinking to yourself, *"I think I need to do this to help me get unstuck,"* and you don't take that action, it just stays in your head as a nice idea. Your transformation can be found at the point of your action. Give it a try.

If you have questions or just want to talk to me about how to meet your grief with a growth mindset, reach out to me. I'm here for you.

Carrie Hopkins-Doubts, MA, PCC, is a spiritual resilience coach supporting people through major life transitions. In 2012, she launched Life's Next Chapter Coaching and is the founder of two other companies, Carrie Hopkins Coaching and Hero Within.

Carrie is an expert in the field of grief recovery and works with people experiencing transition, whether it be in relationships, career, health, or spirituality. She engages clients in discovering and embracing purpose and meaning in their lives by utilizing a potential-based coaching philosophy.

Her passion is helping people reconnect with their hearts, reclaim their power, and re-align with their purpose to create their life's next chapter. She has created a nine-step program, Rebuilding Your Life After Loss.

Carrie earned a Master of Arts in Spiritual Psychology with an emphasis on consciousness, health, and healing, from the University of Santa Monica (USM) in 1998 and a Master of Science in Spiritual Science from Peace Theological Seminary in 2003. She served as the director of education at USM for 20 years.

After studying Psychology, she received her professional coaching certification from the Institute for Professional Excellence in Coaching (iPEC). She is a certified grief counselor by the American Academy of Grief Counseling. Carrie holds the Professional Certified Coach (PCC) credential with International Coaching Federation (ICF) with certifications in mentor coaching, relationship and divorce coaching, and transformational presence coaching.

She has written numerous articles on the subjects of grief, divorce, and transition and is a contributing author for the Huffington Post, The Wellness Universe, SimpleReminders, and Connected Women Magazine.

Carrie is a contributing author of two books: *The Wellness Universe Guide to Complete Self-Care: 25 Tools to Achieve Anything*, and *25 Tools for Goddesses*.

Connect with Carrie:

LNCC Website: https://lifesnextchaptercoaching.com

CHC Website: https://www.carriehopkinscoaching.com

Hero Within Website: https://www.hero-within.com

LinkedIn: https://www.linkedin.com/in/carriedoubts/

Facebook: https://www.facebook.com/LifesNextChapterCoaching

Wellness Universe:
https://www.thewellnessuniverse.com/world-changers/carriedoubts/

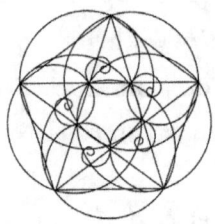

"Feelings are the emotional energy that our thoughts ride on. If we have a thought, we have a feeling to match it. If we keep that energy bottled up, it is harmful. It will either come out in an exaggerated form, or it can go into our tissue cells and become an illness or disease."

~ Carrie Hopkins-Doubts

Chapter 3

HERE WE GO AGAIN

THE PRACTICE OF
RADICAL ACCEPTANCE

Natasha Sharma, BSc, CCHt, DipHB (KGH, UK)

MY STORY

The doors swung wide open revealing boundless abundance and a world of limitless possibilities.

My mind's eye was projecting like a scene out of a science fiction movie.

Sparkling, twinkling vistas were all around me, stretching to infinity in every direction. Pinks, purples, and tiny rainbows sprung out of the iridescent ground; golds, and silver–brilliant crystalline formations making my heart sour, my mind spinning.

My entire body tingled, every cell of my body vibrating faster and faster. I could feel each individual cell, separately and all at once.

The skin of my body felt constrained and stretchy as it strived to keep it all contained.

"Am I dead?" I managed to squeak to my husband.

He looked up at me, the expression on his face a tad amused.

"I think I am going to go to bed and pull the covers over my face and just stay there."

He started laughing.

I was not amused; *I am going to stalk off and burrow deep down into my bed! I mean it!*

I tried to move and realized my legs were not on the same page as my thoughts. In fact, along with seriously wobbly knees, my entire body was doing its own thing, as was my mind and my soul!

Fractured, separate, yet somehow dancing together—weaving this magical experience which I was certain was otherworldly, therefore my earlier conclusion that I was dead.

For sure I never experienced anything remotely like this, in this lifetime at least.

Just a little while earlier I was sitting on the couch contentedly munching my way through a pack of tangy wasabi-flavored crisps and watching TV with my kitty cat snuggled up next to me.

"Babe, can you come here please?" my husband's disembodied voice interrupted my bliss.

Sighing, I reluctantly got up and made my way to his study.

"Can you please show me the breakfast nook references for the architect again?"

As I scrolled through my phone at his request I saw a new email notification, I gave him the references and as I stood there, I flicked open my inbox.

We have launched two days early!

It was an email from my publisher.

How can this be? I am not ready!

Am I now officially a published author? Oh no! I am.

I want to dance with joy! What is happening?

I want to cry. I want to laugh out loud.

I want to scream. Oh Lord, I am shaking!

My cells continued vibrating like this for weeks to come. Even now they feel different than before. I have made many pivots and shifts on my healing and self-awareness journey, but this was different, this was my first fully embodied leveling-up.

Everything is different now. Colors are brighter. I experience, rather than hear music, salt and pepper are all the seasonings I need to create a feast. Rough feels rougher, and soft makes me smile.

And smells! I can navigate the notes of baby powder and cool meadows while lavender, jasmine, and even rose, seem heavy and unnecessarily complex.

Yet the 3D world around me is still the same—daily routine, expectations, obligations, and conversations are dull and mundane with family, and even friends, dragging me down the energy spectrum to dense, sticky lower vibrations.

Fortunately, I'm fully supported by my chosen tribe of powerful women, spiritual warriors, who sing with notes my soul recognizes. They invite me in with open arms, hearts, and minds.

I am seen, recognized, valued, and above all, celebrated.

Working with them, supporting and cherishing them keeps my new reality firmly in place. Here I am, high up on the energy scale; everything is crystal clear—there are no doubts or fears.

Everything is highly charged, my focus, my body, and my voice. I become a channel through which perspective, words, experience, and universal knowledge are available to me intuitively and all at once.

I have not yet mastered how to stay up here all the time. The laws of physics of the third dimension are in play, and whatever goes up must come down.

So, I slide down, the vibrations mellowing with the descent. Swaying in the gentle thrumming of the mid-scale, sticky tendrils of the lowest resonance creep up and slowly drag me below.

At the bottom of the scale, the shadows left behind by healed layers don't miss a beat; they are waiting, arms open, to engulf and swallow me whole. The triggers and the buttons—are ready to be pushed.

Here we go again!

I am paralyzed in my mind. Fed up, tired. How many times must I do this? How do I do this again? Why must I?

There is a pit at the bottom of my stomach that I can't identify, *a feeling of dread perhaps?*

"What is it?" my client asks me as I miss a beat.

"I have a funny feeling. It's a shadow—familiar yet different. More than fear, anticipation, or anxiety, it's almost like I have come to school without my homework.

Actually, as if I know there is an exam tomorrow and I feel I haven't studied enough; I am not prepared."

A lightbulb goes off.

I have up-leveled and feel unprepared!

"I got it! If I stay with the school analogy, it's like being sent to a special class for gifted students! Or made to skip a grade coz I am smart!"

I laugh out loud. I'm loving this analogy.

"Heck, even just like going from one grade to the next! We know we know enough to be here, but it's new. There is so much to learn and do. Can I?"

Can I grow and evolve here? Can I excel, make friends, impress the teachers, and make the environment my own?

Do I have enough knowledge to learn more here?

Will I make the grade?

It brings me immeasurable relief to realize that this is a brand-new layer and not the same cycle of unworthiness repeating.

Cycles—up and down, round and round, over and over again.

The process is the same, but the experience of it is different.

I navigate my way around the shadows. I'm able to shift through and past them faster than ever before.

I'll take this as a win.

The challenge is learning to exist in the 3D world as the new me.

My current mission stays the same. To have conversations about death, openly and often until it becomes an easy, day-to-day dinner table conversation.

To accept that our time here is finite.

To accept that versions of ourselves die and are reborn over and over again through this life until the final curtain falls. We need to pause, reflect, and even grieve for those parts of us and our limited-timed lives until we can fully reach acceptance to move on to the next version of ourselves.

I have written about death and how to use the grieving process to find abundance through accepting death in Chapter 11 of *Wealth Codes: Sacred Strategies for Abundance*. You can buy the book here: https://www.amazon.com/dp/B0BBB4XVBP

After my seismic shift, I'm even more passionate about my passion. I work with people who are deep into self-work and their self-awareness journey. We work together with money and manifestation and the direct relation of this with self-worth, socialization, and conditioning.

I experience my success from the privilege of being a witness to their shifts and leveling up.

Today, as I write this, I have a fresh download to share with you regarding the money story. This is for you if you are a part of our tribe; one who has stepped out of the box to embrace the true purpose of your life.

If you are a lightworker and find yourself often wondering, "I am on the right path, but where is the money? How do I pay the bills? How do I show others the way when my own house isn't in order?"

Q) What is money?

A) Money is energy.

Q) What is energy?

A) Energy is defined as the "ability to do work, which is the ability to exert a force causing displacement of an object." Despite this confusing definition, its meaning is very simple: Energy is just the force that causes things to move. Energy is divided into two types: potential and kinetic.

So, since money is energy (and not merely dollars and cents), it has the force to make things move in our lives.

Now let's imagine this: What if we lived on a planet where we were made up of air instead of water? Where instead of food we could absorb nutrients freely from the air? Where we have the ability to regulate our body temperatures like cats? Thereby needing neither heaters nor air conditioners? Where we had wings to go anywhere, or even teleport there?

What would we need money for then? All our basic needs are met.

However, on this planet, we still have to find and fulfill our purpose. But the transactions are pure energy and not paper or metal representations of it. We would still have to find our tribe. We would need to draw boundaries with people or circumstances that depleted our energy and find purposes and places that filled us up with ecstatic energy, our cups overflowing.

On this planet, we, you and I, light seekers, energy workers, the spiritual warriors would be the wealthiest of them all. Because the energy there is the exact same thing as money here on Earth.

Stay connected (click links in my Bio below). I will be conducting workshops around this soon!

THE PRACTICE

Radical acceptance of who we truly are and surrendering to what is, results in the best and most successful versions of ourselves.

Radical Acceptance + Surrender = Success

We are each unique (like thumbprints and snowflakes), and we all fit together as a mosaic, a tapestry—not a homogeneous blob.

All the facets of our socialization and conditioning are geared toward teaching and training us to believe that we have to *"fit in"* and that if we feel that *"we don't belong,"* it's a bad thing.

It's time to celebrate the fact that we are all different. The exercise I have to share with you is not a standardized representation, but a build-your-own model!

Let's get started:

1. Take a pen/pencil and a piece of paper
2. Draw a straight line, either vertical or horizontal
3. From the following top list, pick a word that resonates the most with you and write it down next to the end of your line
4. From the bottom list, pick a word that resonates the most with you and write it down next to the start of your line

5. Now distribute the remaining words along the line: top down and bottom up.

WORTHINESS ENERGETIC CONTINUUM (WEC)

Top (Tip of and beyond the third dimension) - gratitude, joy, bliss, love, full potential, limitless possibilities, abundance, expansion, courage, fearlessness, faith, confidence, vitality, acceptance, surrender, success

Bottom (The third dimension) - shame, guilt, fear, lack, anger, contraction, helplessness, despair, hopelessness, sadness, blame, sickness, bargaining, worthlessness, doubt, desperation, hustle, failure, disappointment

The increments along the WEC represent the energy of our self-worth. Low at the bottom and high at the top.

Depending on where we spend most of our time vibrationally, the average expresses itself as our self-worth in the present. This impacts all aspects of our life: money, relationships, and health.

Now track and note where *you* spend the most time along the continuum.

What does the higher portion of the WEC remind you of?

To me, it is *a child*.

A return to the pure, pre-conditioned state where anything was possible. We could do and be anything until the world taught us otherwise.

Regardless of which circumstances a child is born into, they all have boundless energy, vivid imaginations, unconditional love, joy, freedom, laughter, and fascination with everything in the world around them.

To them, life on Earth is a magical and wondrous existence that they chose to incarnate into.

As the child grows, their childhood becomes a mixed bag of experiences. What has the maximum impact are the defining moments of crisis, self-worth demolition, and trauma.

In healing work, these moments are what we call "Inner Children." They weave themselves into a template of patterns that are then set for the rest of our lives.

It's possible to map and identify where we are vibrationally and energetically at any point in our life by using the WEC. This realization gives us choice: accept, shift, or surrender.

It's important to remember that this is a scale that we climb up and slide back down until we figure out a way to stay in the state that feels the best to us. So, each of you has to create your own version of hacking the code that will allow you to access the upper frequencies when knocked down.

This is my hack:

Unlocking the Happy Inner Child

As I'm typing, my hand is throbbing with a long-forgotten, but oh-so-familiar spasm. Memories come rushing in.

Hours of handwritten exams resulted in these cramps, as did tedious homework and long essays. The thrum in the muscles of my hand and fingers is accompanied by remembered feelings of accomplishment and joy.

The child me reveled in the pride of a job completed and was not crippled by the angst of the grade to come. She jumped up and shouted, "Finished!"

She was happy to be done, now free to romp and play.

The spams bring a luminous smile to my face as I gently massage around the dull ache in my palm; I'm flooded with a slew of happy memories—of laughter, friendship, school, and shenanigans at recess; my heart space physically feels warm.

So many layers of the self-awareness journey involve old wounds, and I realize today that harnessing the happy child is as important as healing the sad one.

There is a fine line between pleasure and pain.

Sweet pain of a lover's bite with its blinding white light versus the dark, raw pain of trauma, where surrender is pure—a giving in rather than giving up.

In that surrender, we are able to ride along, lifted up to the crest, an orgasm, that allows us a brief glimpse of ecstasy.

Our subconscious mind communicates emotional pain to us through our bodies via injuries, spasms, and diseases. I have realized it is possible to flip it and tap the body, to access memories stored at a cellular level to release positive memories and experiences as well as bad ones.

The circle of life will take us up and back down again, round and back around. Energetically we will slide down the WEC again and again, over and over. The layers and the shadows of the layers, and unhealed bits and pieces will continue drawing us down the scale, as tests or signposts to lessons and answers, I believe as long as we shall live.

We will find ourselves saying over and over, "Here we go again."

The good news is we don't have to stay there! Acceptance that it is what it is, and surrendering to the process makes it possible to move faster through the dense, sticky layers.

This pure joy I am experiencing today feels like a reward from my subconscious mind for a job well done. In response to complete surrender and gratitude. To radical acceptance of what is, for my leveling up.

For the most part of my adult life, these memories were blurred, sometimes surfacing and coming in on the high notes of a well-remembered song and then vanishing like the whiff of my grandmother's kitchen.

To use one's hands is a somatic experience. In therapy, we encourage writing and journaling with pen and paper. Handwriting is an ideo-motor response, straight from the subconscious mind—muscle memory and everything that goes along with it.

Laptops and phones have replaced pen and paper. Evolution is a good thing, but now, even if I do pick up a pen, it's usually just to sign something or quickly jot things down. I know I'm giving away my age as I type this!

Today I'm triggered by something good for a change. It delights my heart space to say the word "trigger" for something positive.

So, what's my point?

How did my hand start hurting in the first place?

What did I do to bring about this beautiful download?

I was coloring!

Yes! Coloring in a coloring book for grown-ups!

Coloring with intention and focus.

Coloring until the picture was complete.

The reward was this.

How blessed I am!

I first came across this a few years ago when it was all the rage. I could not grasp the concept of coloring for grown-ups being a tool for mindfulness, relaxation, and therapy.

Somebody gave me a hardbound coloring book of intricate mosaics at that time. The only reason I never regifted it was because the cover was bejeweled and beautiful. *Maybe there is something to it? Perhaps I will use it?*

It lay gathering dust.

A few days ago, I was ordering a bunch of stuff online and needed some Sharpies for labeling. I got a bit carried away and ordered a whole bunch of colors—neon and metallics too!

After they arrived and I finished off my work, I felt like doing more with them.

The colors were so pretty!

I remembered that there was a coloring book somewhere, so I dug it out.

Then I ordered more colors—pencils, paints, crayons, and pastels.

And a fancy electric sharpener (I always wanted one of those!).

When the deliveries arrived, I was like a child on Christmas morning.

It took a couple of days to fully engage with the activity.

I remembered the way to color inside the lines, the anticipation of which color to use next. There was a feeling of accomplishment when the coloring was complete with no mistakes (well, maybe a few).

Perhaps I've been coloring outside the box for so long I had forgotten the joy of craftsmanship.

Of precision.

Of the magic in colors.

Of the hypnotic freedom of thought that ensues when we're so focused on a task that our mind is free to roam the universe and laugh at the side of Source and marvel at creation.

If you don't have a coloring book at hand, and are inspired to do some coloring yourself straight away, I have a few sheets for you that you can print off right now. Along with some other gifts for you:

https://www.mind-bodyspeak.com/mindset-mastery/

Ultimately you need to discover for yourself, which activity will unlock your happy inner child. Try and pick something that involves the hands or the full body. If nothing else, there is always music! Good old retro tunes that your parents listened to on happy days!

Here are some ideas to get you started:

Clay modeling

Lego/block building

Playing a musical instrument

Finger painting

Jungle gym/climbing

Dancing

Running in circles when you go for your morning run/hike

Spinning round and round (twirling)

Hula hoop

Swinging on the swing

Trampoline

Anything that you enjoyed in your childhood—try picking it up again as an adult and watch the magic unfold!

**Natasha Sharma** is a speaker, author, and mentor. She was born and brought up in the United Kingdom. She lives in Mumbai, India with her husband Rrajeev Sharma, and their two feline fur babies, Freyja and Isaac. She is a bonus mother to the beautiful Rewa Khare Sharma.

In Human Design, she is a Mental Projector with a 3/5 Profile. Created to be a vehicle of wisdom, a guide for the people who need her. Who are ready for her, who recognize her, and invite her into their lives simply for the words she has to share and the questions she will inevitably ask, for she perceives.

Natasha means resurrection and her spirit animal shows up alternately as the snake or the turtle. Precious spirits of Earth and of Water. Divine, ancient, feminine powerful energy. She embodies the healing powers of the self, birth, death, shedding, and rebirth—of transformation, self-realization, and radical acceptance.

No surprise her expertise is guiding people to cure themselves of physical injuries and diseases by exploring the metaphysical connection of the mind-body-soul to the said illness or malcontent.

Effortlessly traversing the conscious and subconscious realms for her own growth and that of the people she works with.

Holding spaces, with wisdom, divinely blessed insights, sensitivity, love, and above all joy.

Nothing gives her more power than the gratitude she experiences through being witness to the transformation of others.

Natasha has some gifts for you as thank you for reading the chapter.

It includes an introduction to Human Design and a discount coupon code for your own reading with a Human Design Expert and much more!

https://www.mind-bodyspeak.com/mindset-mastery/

Connect with Natasha:

Email: natasha@mind-bodyspeak.com

Website: https://www.mind-bodyspeak.com

Facebook: https://www.facebook.com/BodySpeak.in/

Instagram: https://www.instagram.com/bodyspeak.in/

LinkedIn: https://www.linkedin.com/in/bodyspeak/

Clubhouse: https://www.clubhouse.com/@natasha.sharma

On Amazon: https://www.amazon.com/author/natasha.sharma

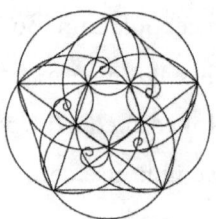

"I'm fully supported by my chosen tribe of powerful women, spiritual warriors, who sing with notes my soul recognizes. They invite me in with open arms, hearts, and minds. I am seen, recognized, valued, and above all, celebrated."

~ Natasha Sharma

Chapter 4

POWERFUL LESSONS FROM LIFE'S POTHOLES

5 SUBTLE SHIFTS TOWARD A HEALTHY MINDSET

Colleen Avis, Life Coach, Mindfulness Guide

MY STORY

"Slow down, Colleen, you are going to crash!" Fear-filled screeching, my mom yelling, flailing her arms, in distress at what she could see unfolding before her. "Oh my God, Colllleeeeeen, Slow down. Colleen. Slow. Down!"

A calm voice, secure and unwavering in my mind, *Slow down?! Come on Mom, really, no way! Seriously, I know what I am doing, and there are hot cookies and chocolate milk waiting for me. See ya there Mom.*

Like a Tour de France rider, I pedaled harder, like every time we rode our bikes down the dirt road to visit my great-grandmother. I did all things in life fast. I prided myself on always arriving first. It was fun, and most days, even decades later, I prefer the excitement of some speed in my life. It gets the heart pumping, although I do realize now that it means I typically miss a few vital details.

There wasn't much my mom could have said or done to slow my pace. A girl and her bike—I was on top of the world, untouchable, at an unconscious pace, enjoying every moment of my freedom, wind in my hair, and giggling all the way. I turned to look at my mom. She looked like she was miles behind me, and I chose not to listen to her.

At this pace, I wasn't listening to much, including my own tiny and faint voice, the voice my body would've appreciated me hearing. If I had listened, I might have heard, *Are you thinking this through? I mean, all the potholes? Be sure to dodge well, or you are going down hard!*

Looking at my hands and knees, gravel replaced space where there once was flesh. The deeply embedded particles of the oil-treated dirt road and stones either removed my skin altogether, or found their way deeply embedded beneath it. Which, at that moment, I thought would remain there permanently.

A deep purplish red, warm thick blood gushed down my shins filling my socks and shoes. It was a full-speed pothole-induced wipeout, the one my mom saw in my future and tried to warn me of. And now the sound of tears streaming down my face. Okay, maybe it was full-on screaming and hysteria.

The walk home, uphill the entire way, pushing my 1970s solid metal frame one-speed bike that I'm sure was a four-time hand-me-down and at least a size too big for me, was unexpected, frustrating, and painful. I mean, I was ten years old.

The backcountry road was dirt and gravel and loaded with potholes, just like it was every spring. Upstate New York winters were bitterly cold, and most days included tons of snow and ice falling from the gray overcast skies. The winter freeze-thaw effects, coupled with the springtime melting, created the perfect recipe for potholes. It was somewhat of a game, even in a car, to dodge the rim-bending, suspension-eating craters that seemed to breed like the rabbits each spring.

Crying and bruised ego in check, the walk home gave my mom plenty of time to impress upon me why going that fast was not a good idea and that I should know better and be looking to avoid the potholes.

When we arrived home from the wipeout, I did my best to sit still in the tub, soaking my sore body as she scrubbed and picked the gravel dirt road from my flesh—lifting skin flaps and disinfecting the wounds with the burn of rubbing alcohol.

THE SPACE BETWEEN THE POTHOLES

Forty years later, I still bear the scars of that bike wipeout. Honestly, the scar on my left knee could use plastic surgery, and I'm confident there are still pieces of gravel in my hands. But I treasure all the adventures, journeys, and lessons I experienced while spending my childhood on pothole-filled dirt roads. I wouldn't change a thing because most days didn't include any massive wipeout.

Dry, warm days meant billowing dust balls spinning off the road and lingering even when the cars were long gone. The oil sprayed on the road helped control the dust storms, but it also added a pitch-black smoky petroleum-like smell and sticky tar-like material that forever attached itself to the cars.

My summer "tan" was really dust and dirt sticking to my legs between the top of my multi-color tube socks and the bottom of my cut of jean shorts. I can still feel the exhaustion in my body and the smile on my face as I stood in the shower after a great day outside, watching the brown water wash down the drain.

Wet days meant dust was traded for mud and road runoff. Cold days meant freezing and thawing, the true creators of more potholes and loose gravel.

A typical day was biking quiet dirt roads from sunrise to sunset, and traveling to my best friend's farm, where we played barn hide and seek. Or to my favorite nature spot, where I simply wandered and tried to get lost, or to the local pond, where I searched for newts and other critters.

The spaces and places between each pothole, sticky tar, and dust storm are where all my best memories happened. These spaces sometimes required skillful navigation, but it was fun, high adventure, and something I wouldn't trade for the world.

Sure, many days I wiped out and then wiped out again. On other days I wiped out, cleaned out my wounds, and got right back on my bike. Somedays, I rode safely past each pothole, avoiding them altogether because I knew exactly where they were.

POTHOLES ARE A GUARANTEE

Like Upstate New York potholes, it's dirty and messy to navigate life's potholes. And while not always done gracefully or well, being wiped out by them has provided me with my greatest life learnings. After my skin-removing bike wipeout, I did attempt to slow down and take better notice of the holes in the road. And after eating the dirt kicked up by passing cars on many occasions, I did learn to be more aware of what was coming down the road and step off to the side of the road or at least cover my eyes, nose, and mouth. When I chose to be aware, each pothole gave me a new possibility and opportunity.

I could choose to take a new direction and expand and grow - or not.

We all have the ability to choose a new direction and expand or not. We have the ability to choose to hit the same pothole over and over and continue down the same road, or to make a shift, change direction, mend the pothole or simply focus on the journey and space between each one, lessening the damage they can create when we encounter them.

My childhood skinned knee wipeout was not a major life-altering pothole. Although it was a pothole I chose to avoid a second time—believe me, I never wiped out like that again! And it did offer me a lifelong lesson on the value of slowing down, listening, and a reminder to embrace the beauty in life's smallest journeys.

Potholes as adults, I think we would all agree, feel scarier, higher risk, just bigger, or mandatory to hide from ourselves and the world. *Colleen, they won't accept you; you aren't enough; you don't fit in.* That is the voice of my adult pothole. Actually, it has taken decades to hear and listen to that voice, honor her and work not to ignore her but rather, choose to lean into what she is meant to teach me. Choosing to expand was not my first step in the journey. First, I spent years falling into that pothole and trying to get back out. *Oh, the pain of the figurative road rash and burn experienced during that journey. Colleen, how many years will you spend picking gravel from this wound?*

Let's just say this adult pothole has required more time and attention than "recovering" from my bike wipeout. And yet I wouldn't change a thing because I now choose with clarity and curiosity to be aware and take intentional action to create and cultivate the mindset I know is best for me. It's not always easy, but subtle shifts paired with my desire to live my best life make it all worth it!

So why not cultivate attention to how you respond to what life deals you? Easier said than done, and we know it is. So, choose to embrace subtle shift mindset practices—because you too can climb out of the pothole and live your best life.

THE PRACTICE

My pothole story is meant to offer some nostalgia, a moment to revisit a life experience you had where you giggled, or appreciate the growth you experienced from a personal pothole. It doesn't reflect my most challenging, heartbreaking moment in life—that story is in my book, *Sacred Spaces: Subtle Shifts for Mind, Body, and Home Transformation*—yet even the smallest pothole in life gives us wisdom.

Let's be honest, some obstacles are bigger than others and take greater time to heal. Being passed over for a promotion may feel more stressful than getting stuck in traffic or your child getting one poor test grade. A skinned knee from a bike wipeout may be a minor bump, yet offer a powerful heart-filling childhood memory that reminds you to always look for the good in life.

When life deals us a pothole, a forced pause in our life's progression, I invite you not to get stuck there. Rather choose to explore how challenges can also propel you forward. Subtle shift mindset practices can move you from stuck to thriving and support you in responding to challenges where you may have previously snapped, felt broken, or reacted in a way you would wish you hadn't.

Mindset mastery can be fun when taken with gentleness toward yourself. Your current mindset wasn't created in a day, and it may take some time to shift. So, I invite you to start where you are and practice subtle shifts that feel natural.

Let me know which ones worked best for you, and if you need additional examples and practices for any of the shifts below, you can find them here: https://subtle-shifts.com

MEDITATION IS A MUST

There is no other way to say this. Meditation is your greatest mindset tool. I hear you: "I have a busy mind, and it won't settle long enough to meditate, and I just can't meditate." I have heard it all, and I'm here to throw the BS flag on it.

You can meditate. I have helped all my clients who "could not meditate" meditate daily. It's now a non-negotiable for them. Not to mention, there are more scientific studies than potholes in Upstate New York that prove daily meditation practices focus you on the present moment, guide you toward less judgment, improve memory, and reduce stress.

If you want to shift your mindset, you must create a sense of calm, peace, and harmony in your life. Meditation is the tool to empower this. The benefits of meditation go way beyond the moments you're practicing it and teach you to respond versus react and lead with compassion, greater focus, awareness, and creativity.

Start now and immediately shift into a healthier mindset.

- Sit comfortably.
- Bring your awareness to your feet, and with each inhale, imagine drawing breath through the bottom of your feet.
- Let each inhale ground you and connect your mind and body with the stability and safety of the earth.
- Let each exhale settle your mind and body, softening and relaxing as the earth supports you.
- Spend as much time as you like in this practice, and when it is complete, continue with your day.

POSITIVE AFFIRMATIONS

Positive affirmations challenge the negative thoughts guaranteed to come your way. So, each day, share affirmations with yourself that communicate what and how you want to live. Repeat them to yourself regularly, and say them like they're already happening.

Choose in this practice to be positive and release self-doubt and negative self-talk. You deserve to shift from negative internal messages to inspiring and motivating ones.

Here are a few daily affirmations to consider; use one or create your own:

- Today I choose happiness and peace
- I am enough
- I trust that what I need I have within me
- I am grateful for my physical body
- I know how to do this

Consistently start your day with this practice and notice what shifts in your life.

GROUNDING AND EARTHING

Some call it grounding, some call it earthing, and I call it a "whole being reset and harmonizer." In an article from the Earthing Institute focused on the earthing effects on PTSD, experts state that "grounding has a natural defusing effect on stress. It reduces inflammation and related chronic pain. It improves blood flow, improves sleep, energy, and mood."

This "whole being reset and harmonizer" changes the activity in the brain, shifting it from overloaded to calm. Simply put, grounding is when we place our feet (or any body part) on the ground and connect to Mother Earth. During this connection, our bodies naturally absorb negative electrons from the earth, which improves our overall vitality (and so much more!)

I have personally been intentionally grounding for over seven years. Since then, grounding has supported my mental and physical well-being. It has been a direct contributor to reducing inflammation, stress, and fatigue in my mind and body.

Given your mindset is affected by all your spaces—mind, body, and home—you can use grounding to positively affect your mind and body, allowing it to improve your mood and overall mindset. A healthy mind and body are indeed a healthy mindset.

REFRAME YOUR THOUGHTS

According to Dr. Deepak Chopra, humans have around 60,000 – 80,000 thoughts a day. Of those thoughts, approximately 90% are recycled and negative thoughts from the day before.

The good news is you can practice shifting those thoughts to be more productive and in support of a healthier mindset through the practice of reframing. Here are a few quick shifts to try:

- Be aware of your thoughts and what they are saying to you. Is what you hear serving you? Most of us go through life without ever tuning in to notice our thoughts, and yet this simple practice can be very powerful and is the first step to reframing.

- Explore balancing negative thoughts and replacing them with positive and supportive thoughts. For example, on a rainy day, you may find yourself thinking: *Ugh, another rainy day. I hate the rain!* A balancing thought may be: *Another rainy day allows me the time to make a home-cooked meal for my family.* Or: *This rain will be good for the garden. I'll spend this rainy day catching up on a few outstanding house jobs.*

- Be understanding when your negative thoughts are a result of things you can't control. Consider how you may reframe your thoughts by accepting that potholes are inevitable and that the obstacle may offer you an opportunity or growth.

When we reframe our negative thoughts to positive ones, we are empowering ourselves to generate new ideas, be creative and open ourselves to more possibilities, building resilience and a healthier mindset.

CREATE A PERSONAL SACRED SPACE

Take time daily to be in your favorite place! If only for a few minutes, enjoy time with yourself, with your thoughts, and pause. This daily pause allows you to reconnect with yourself, turn up the volume on your inner voice, and recognize what it is that you may need or want in specific areas of your life.

I'm passionate about helping people see the sacredness in all the spaces they live in—mind, body, and home. So, for this mindset practice, create for yourself a space you want to be in—a physical space where you can get away from the busyness of life and the demands of others.

This is not about getting your entire house in order; this is about making a subtle shift and creating even the smallest corner of your home to be your go-to sacred space. When our physical space is free of clutter and distraction, our minds are invited to follow.

Create a clutter-free, comfortable, relaxed, and inspired space just for you.

MASTERY NOT REQUIRED

Your mindset can be challenging to shift, not to mention master. However, we know thanks to the science of neuroplasticity and an individual's desire to shift to a healthier mindset, even the most stubborn lifelong habits, belief systems, and life potholes can truly change.

As you explore the above subtle shifts, get curious about what works for you, what suits your daily life, and where you think you can really be consistent with one or two practices. Be honest with yourself, and rather than trying to do it all or analyze what will work or not work, simply start.

Make one shift toward your goals. Procrastination and ignoring potholes and obstacles in life do not heal wounds, help us get our needs met, or begin to shift a mindset.

And remember, the adventure and joy that happens between all the potholes in life far outweigh the actual potholes, if you choose to live life that way.

LET'S CONNECT

These mindset shifts are ones I practice daily. They are non-negotiable for me. My intention is to practice so I get better at practicing.

Of course, there are days when it's hard to hold myself accountable—those are the days I call my life coach. I'd love to hear from you and learn how your mindset shifts toward your well-being are working for you. Connect with me to share or co-create and support each other.

I'd love for you to join my free 7-day subtle shifts practices here http://subtle-shifts.com/7-day-challenge. And you can always connect with me live by setting up a free discovery call here: www.subtle-shifts.com.

Colleen Avis is the author of the award-winning book *Sacred Spaces, Subtle Shifts for Mind, Body, and Home Transformation* (Volumes One and Two), a certified Chopra life coach, and Ayurveda and mindfulness mentor. She has spent the last decade guiding clients to create spaces they love to live in—mind, body, and home, and embraces the whole person.

She is passionate about supporting others in their journey to live a harmonious life. Colleen guides her clients toward wholeness and purpose while untangling limiting beliefs, unhealthy patterns, and unconscious conditions.

Her clients say working with Colleen feels like being gently guided toward their own wisdom. And that she helps them see the opportunity and transformation in stories once viewed with frustration, fear, and disappointment.

It all starts with meeting clients where they are now and knowing that subtle shifts create impactful and sustainable transformation. Building their unique wellness toolkit is at the core of her approach and is proven through her personal and clients' experiences.

Her approach is holistic, unique, non-judgmental, and offers an informed perspective. Colleen knows her most powerful tools are the ones she has integrated into her life over the last decade by transforming through her own experiences and openly bringing her life lessons, struggles, and transformative tools to her clients.

In addition to her Chopra certifications, Colleen is a yoga teacher, integrative NLP practitioner, and studying to complete her SOMA Breathe Holistic Health Coach Certification.

Colleen lives in McLean, Virginia, with her husband, son, and their dog. She is happiest walking in the woods and losing track of time, on the sidelines of her son's lacrosse games cheering him on, trying to better her golf handicap without losing patience, and eating dark chocolate-covered almonds without accidentally eating too many.

Connect with Colleen:

Website: www.subtle-shifts.com

Instagram: @colleen_avis_bewell

Books: https://subtle-shifts.com/about/#book

"There is no other way to say this.
Meditation is your greatest mindset tool."

~ Colleen Avis

Chapter 5

EVERYTHING'S A CHOICE

HOW TO CRAWL OUT OF THE PIT OF DESPAIR AND THRIVE

Star Studonivic

MY STORY

The sheet clings to my clammy, sweaty body. My neck feels like there's a noose tightening around it. Anxiety roils through me. I'm panting as if I've just run up a long hill, and it hurts. *It must have been a bad dream.*

I roll over and shut my eyes. I unclench my aching jaws. No relief from the overriding feeling something is terribly wrong. I dismiss it and brush it away as if it were an annoying blood-sucking mosquito.

A persistent ache in my shoulder creates a freeway for pain. Uninvited! *Am I a character in a B-grade horror movie? What kind of dream is this?* My heart flutters like an angry bird in too small a cage. *What the crap? Go away. I want to sleep!*

Ample moonlight leads me into the living room without turning on any lights. Movement feels as if my pajamas are a soggy wet weight pulling me into an undertow. Breath is stingy. I feel like I'm trying to breathe through a straw. My partner, Larry, joins me. Three nitro pills later nothing has changed. *It's okay. It will go away.* It didn't.

The 3:00 a.m. trip to the ER is fast (Larry could double for Andretti any time). Bright lights and measured voices. Questions. A quick jab to insert an IV. My insides are hyper alert, but my actions can't match the cadence. My head hurts. The monitor I'm tethered to shows a pattern resembling the Dow Jones Industrial Average of 2020. Where's the nice steady rhythm? After swallowing water and a small aspirin, my stomach rebels at the intrusion. *It's just because I'm not used to drinking water at this hour.*

I'm good at believing my own bullshit. Waves of anxiety battle waves of nausea. Sporadic aching crawls down both shoulders and settles in my back. *Maybe this is just a bad dream.* Denial once again takes center stage.

The harsh reality slams my consciousness like a stinging slap across the face. By now I'd been admitted to the cardiac unit (for a couple of days) and had already been through a multitude of tests. Still hooked up to tubes, as the A-Fib was not under control, I was given the news that surgery was mandatory if I wanted to continue living. I needed bypass surgery, a carotid endarterectomy (a polite term for slitting your throat), and possibly some other procedures.

I'm informed, very gently, I will be on a heart/lung machine for an extended period. "We need to stop your heart so we can fix it. The machine will take over breath and circulation." "So that means you'll hold my heart in your hands?" "In a manner of speaking, yes. Your heart needs to stop so we can do the bypass and any other procedures necessary." I stop breathing for a few moments. I try to feel what it's like to pause between heartbeats and what that will be like for a long period of time. *Is this what it's like to experience death? Where do I go while the machine keeps me alive without my heartbeat?*

Masking sheer terror I calmly agree and smile. I don't want Larry to know how scared I am. Rescheduling allows the surgery to take place soon—November third, election day. *That's the day after tomorrow. How do I prepare for this? What do I do?* If all fails, try some humor. "How about you promise me good results for both the surgery and the election since they are occurring at the same time?" The doctor smiles at me and his eye contact is intense. There is a steadfast gaze of assurance, confidence, and additional energy of humbleness. It surprises me. "We will give you our best." He includes his entire team in this statement.

The night prior, a blood transfusion ensures a "juicier" (surgeon's exact word!) entry into surgery. *Who are you? Why did you donate your blood? Did you know it would make this big a difference?*

Somehow, I feel this foreign blood strengthen my weak system. I'm going into this surgery as strong as possible. My body feels stronger. My spirits don't. *Whoever you are, thank you for becoming part of me. Thank you for giving me the strength I don't have. I have no reserves. You're my reserve.*

My friend and Reiki mentor organizes a Reiki circle by phone. It dials down the anxiety from sheer terror to frightened. Very frightened. But this circle and the knowledge these very special people in my life are in my corner, along with close friends and chosen family, carries me into the operating theater confidently. It will be a command performance. I have a great surgeon, his assistants, and a reassuring anesthesiologist. I want to live.

Awakening in the ICU, I remember the hum of a tuning fork vibrating in my ear (an excellent suggestion from my Reiki mentor who is also a vibrational sound master). Taking a painful breath, I descend back into a deep, black warm abyss. I'm too exhausted to do anything, but I hope I'm still alive. Strains of words from "Hotel California" echo inside my head: "This could be heaven or this could be hell."

It's the first night out of the ICU. I'm restless and uncomfortable. The mask covering my face is tightly sealed around the edges invoking an unreal sensation of swimming and breathing in the dense, murky air. A deep breath is impossible. Any breath is a struggle and takes 100 percent of my effort. I encourage myself. *Just another breath. That's all it is. You can do this. You're not trapped. You're safe. You survived.* Waves of icy fear creep up my spine. I can't move my head; the neck incision hurts too much. I can't move my arms. The inside of my leg is sore and I remember it's the leg from which they used some of my veins for the bypass. My biggest challenge is to acknowledge the nurse's instructions not to move.

A tear edges its way around the rim of my mask as absolute panic engulfs me. Adrenaline surges into flight or fight mode. The urge to rip the mask off and shred it intensifies until I realize I can barely breathe, let alone move. My self-pity party is interrupted by a calm, clear voice of an extraordinary cardiac nurse who lingers by my side. "You're doing just fine. Everything went well." Her voice is soothing. I need more than words. I feebly move my fingers in an attempt to reach for her hand. I look into her eyes and beg for reassurance with my look. Message received. Her hand gently enfolds mine. I relax.

Fast forward 11 days to the journey home. Moving from a wheelchair to the back seat of the car expends marathon effort. I learn I get to be "Miss Daisy" for a couple of months and a licensed backseat driver as it's too dangerous to sit in a front seat that has an airbag. The thought of anything touching my chest creates instant panic.

I'm home. The oxygen tube constantly tangles around my bandaged neck, which hurts. I feel like one big bruise. I'm struggling to breathe even with oxygen. I can't move well as I must be on my back and semi-upright— no rolling to one side as the clips holding my breastbone together might shift. There is a bandage covering an incision that carves the front of my body in half. *Why? Why did this happen? I'm a yoga teacher. I eat well. I'm a Reiki Master. I try so hard to do everything right. Why me?*

A voice inside counters: *Why not you?* I'm not having it! I'm angry. I'm tired. I hurt. *This isn't fair. I didn't sign up for this.* Succumbing to sleep my thoughts tumble over one another. Black fear creeps over me and stifles me in its embrace.

It's 3:00 a.m. Again. Apparently, this is my own personal prime time. Still on the couch, as that's the only comfortable location, the lights are on, but dim. I can't stand darkness. There's plenty of time for thought. It's all I can do. My mind can wander but my body can't. My parents both died from heart failure. My dad at 60, and my mother at the exact same age I am 73. They died. I lived. Why?

I come to the realization I'm not afraid of dying. I'm afraid of not living.

Note: Most people undergoing this surgery have a fear of darkness for a while after the surgery. It's attributed to deep anesthesia and time on a heart/lung machine. There are periods of "Swiss cheese" mind where it feels as if there are holes in your memory. There is paranoia about listening and feeling a different rhythm of your heartbeat. Hearing can be hyper-sensitive. There are changes in taste and appetite. There's nausea. Most of these reactions diminish after a while.

EVERYTHING'S A CHOICE | 53

THE PRACTICE

"Sometimes when you're in a dark place you think you've been buried, but you've actually been planted."

~ Christine Caine

Giving yourself a chance is a self-gift. All the offers of help in the world will not match what you give yourself. Start there. Give yourself the opportunity to craft your future and give yourself grace. Above all, give yourself patience. And ample time.

Start with the most basic action life offers: breath. It is indeed life, and it's prana—not just breath. It's the beginning. Life starts with breath and ends with no breath. Choose.

Once you acknowledge your breath, begin to examine it. How deep is the inhale? Is it smooth or ragged? Does it have rough edges? Can you calm it? Smooth the breath out by making it as even as possible and directing it into your belly bowl. This calms your parasympathetic nervous system which is essential to your physical being and state of mind. They are equally important.

If you are immobile and in pain, find a location on your body that doesn't hurt. Take your attention there and direct your inhale to nourish, and your exhale to move the energy of "no pain" from its home to a path outside that area. Each inhale brings in what you need, and each exhale moves "no pain" energy farther away from its origin. Give the breath a color. Give it a temperature to your liking. Know it's alive and is a healing energy. This prana is vibrant, healing, nurturing, and a sacred gift.

Do an honest assessment of where you are emotionally, spiritually, mentally, and physically, as each has merit. If you're on medication, research it and become knowledgeable about what you're putting into your body. Food is essential. Good nutrition is medicine. Create a schedule for simple activities. Movement is paramount, even if it's very little. Find something to look forward to every day. Begin engaging with your world. Self-pity is best at a low dosage. Feel it. Whine. And leave it behind. That was then. You have a now and a future. What will you do with it?

Take a good look in the mirror. Look at your reflection with eyes of kindness. Not judgment. Promise yourself you will treat yourself as well as you would your best friend. Learn to be nice to yourself. Honest, but supporting and nice. Become your own best friend. Use tools offered to you. In my case it was home health, and after a while, cardiac rehab. I was blessed to have fellow Reiki practitioners offer Reiki and was anointed with oils and received tuning fork sessions. Resist the urge to compete with yourself, but begin setting realistic goals. Avoid being a self-pitying couch potato. Meet your goals. Chart them. Methodically increase them. Journal.

Pray. Acknowledge your progress and know it's the foundation for improving every aspect of your life. Be amazed at your progress. Be amazed you're alive and breathing. Find the humor in your situation: Mine was directing an imaginary yoga class while entering the room using a walker in my oh so colorful well-worn pajamas.

Once you begin to heal, the momentum kicks in. Your body and mind are miraculous. Be grateful. Begin expanding your dreams and the what ifs. Map your way there. You can do it. You can become a better version of yourself, filled with much more empathy, compassion, gentleness, and love. Use your experiences to refine your skills.

Glance in your rear-view mirror. Take a deep breath. Your past led you to the life you have now. Use and polish the tools you've gathered along this journey. You matter. There's a reason you're alive. Make this life extraordinary! Know you can. You are your own gift. Never forget life is precious; you're part of this intricate, pulsating, beautiful web. And you belong.

Star is a Reiki Master and certified yoga instructor. Her yoga specialties are primal movement (which can be done seated), seated yoga, restorative yoga, and basic fundamental yoga. Her classes are particularly designed for those who are movement challenged. Primal movement is based upon Annie Adamson's Primal Vinyasa - https://primalvinyasayoga.com. She has regained and improved her pre-surgery fitness level. Life is good!

Star's most humbling experience (and there have been many) was with a student who is a wheelchair bound quadriplegic whose reason for attending class was simply because class enabled her to breathe easier and know she was part of a community and accepted. She taught the entire class about connection.

Star also uses tuning forks, essential oils, and crystals to assist in Reiki sessions as well as ritual work. Her ritual work is tailored to the needs of her client. She is also a calligrapher and artist.

Connect with Star:

For your own personal ancestor messages, please contact her directly at studonivic@gmail.com.

Website: www.studonivic.com.

"You matter. There's a reason you're alive. Make this life extraordinary! Know you can. You are your own gift. Never forget life is precious; you're part of this intricate, pulsating, beautiful web. And you belong."

~ Star Studonivic

Chapter 6

RADICAL RESPONSIBILITY

TAKING BACK DOMINION OVER YOUR STORY TO CREATE YOUR HEAVEN ON EARTH

Seth Rohrer

MY STORY

"If you can't tell me right now that we're going to be good for the rest of our lives and never talk about divorce again, then you have to let me go!"

It's only been four months! How am I supposed to know if everything will be good forever?

I sat there on the phone with my stomach doing somersaults in my belly, as my world was fixing to come crashing down.

"Can we have this conversation when I get home?"

"**No!** I need to know now."

Is she really going to make me do this right now, over the phone?

Another ultimatum laid before me, but this time was different. I had reached the end of my rope. I could no longer deny myself appeasing her.

"I can't promise you that," I said, with a heavy-hearted resolve knowing full well what this would mean.

We had spent the previous five months "working" on our marriage. The topic of divorce had come up after an intense conversation about my refusal to adopt a child, but what that conversation did was bring to light the fact that I had been unhappy for years.

As we got off the phone that night, I sat with the idea of our impending divorce. Even with the load of logistical issues to attend to, I felt a huge weight removed from my shoulders.

Our 14 years had come with moves to four different states across the country seeking a college education and job satisfaction. We brought two beautiful children into the world, and due to my rotating schedule as a firefighter, I had the privilege of being their primary caregiver.

For the last couple of years, my work to survive had seemingly been just about to turn into our time to thrive, but just as the light would begin to shine at the end of the tunnel, my wife's medical issues flared up.

"I'm sick of going to doctors! I just don't have the energy anymore," she said as we discussed what to do about her not feeling good. Inconsistencies became the norm. Her health often prevented my planned activities, but much less often hers.

"That's just not an option!" I responded with exacerbation in my voice. "You still don't feel right, so you don't get to just stop trying to heal yourself."

"I can't do it anymore!"

You committed to "in sickness and in health." You can't leave someone because they get sick. This is what you signed up for, so just suck it up and figure out how to make it work.

This was the first time I remember these words running through my mind. It was obvious I was not happy. What do you do when you're not happy with your marriage, and you've told yourself your whole life that divorce isn't an option?

Change your scenery, of course!

We moved across town. I went bigger. Society teaches us that bigger is better and better equals more happiness. Big house. Big yard. Big shop. Big pool.

Yeah! This will do it. I can be happy here regardless of my wife's desire or ability to go out and adventure. This is going to be great!

Spoiler alert!

It didn't work.

It did bring temporary distraction with more survival tasks to keep my mind occupied and my attention on things other than my relationship.

After my wife returned from a weeklong business trip, I came to the grave realization that it was easier to manage and live life without her, even with two kids.

"Seth, can you get me a drink?"

"Seth, can you get me something to eat?"

"Can you deal with the kids? I just don't have the energy to get up."

I accepted this as part of her medical issues. *One day we will get this shit figured out and then life will be great!* I thought to myself many times.

It was a warm day in early summer; I was covered in mud fixing the sprinkler system and my phone rang.

"I need your help!" she said. I hurried inside to see what was wrong.

"Can you get something to drink? I don't feel good, and I can't get up."

Rage grew inside as I stared at her laying on the couch.

"Really?! I am in the middle of a big project that requires me to crawl under the house, and you call me to drop everything to come get you a drink?"

I became accustomed to taking care of the kids and the house by myself most of the time, but this was too far. She wouldn't even fend for herself long enough for me to get a couple of hours of work done.

After 13-plus years together, I had to face a new reality. This was not a fleeting moment that would pass. This was likely the rest of my life, so how was I going to make this work?

My perception began to shift.

I don't know if I can do this anymore. This is not a partnership. Maybe divorce is an option.

As you are aware by now, we did divorce.

For a while, I used this to torture myself. *How could I have let this happen? What happened to "til death do us part"? Why am I feeling this deep sense of loss when I know I wasn't happy? How will this affect my kids?*

I came to realize it had nothing to do with her health. I was unhappy because I wasn't authentic with my wife or myself. I created a story that she never agreed to.

I was giving my power away by silencing my own voice and choking back my truth. I was living a life that didn't bring me joy, which is a half-ass life at best!

With the simple truth of radical responsibility, I began creating my life to reflect the wonderful dream of my own heaven. Step by step. One choice at a time. One shifted perception at a time. One inspired action at a time.

I have since chosen different perspectives, allowing me to rewrite this story of my first marriage to one that brings me gratitude and compassion. No more being the victim of circumstance.

THE PRACTICE

RADICAL RESPONSIBILITY

You are giving away your power and creating the half-ass life you are living!

"Who the hell are you to tell me that," you're probably saying right now. This is not an accusation or judgment. This is a moment of realization.

Before you get pissed off and throw the book, read that again.

You're giving away your power and creating the half-ass life you're living.

I did it for years. I didn't know I was giving my power away, but that doesn't change the fact that I was. Let's dive deeper.

How does that statement feel to you?

Not, what did you think when you read that?

How does that feel?

Sit with it for a second without any judgment on you, me, or your life.

Are you taking radical responsibility for your life?

If you're like most people (and me), you believe you already take responsibility for your life. I certainly did.

What does radical responsibility really mean?

"Take responsibility for your actions," I can still hear my dad say.

"If you say you're gonna do something for someone, you better do it," or at least make sure it gets done.

This was my idea of responsibility.

However, if you say things like, "I can't. . .", "I have to. . ." or "There's no other choice," you're letting your circumstances control you, and you're giving away your power to create your beautiful story.

Years after my divorce, I started seeking answers and one of my mentors asked this question.

"Are you taking responsibility in your life?"

Absolutely. I don't know very many people who are more responsible than I am.

- *I fess up regardless of the consequences.*
- *I'm willing to face whatever consequences come my way based on my actions.*
- *I'm willing to make executive decisions and deal with the outcome head-on.*
- *Yes, I take responsibility in my life.*

"I'll bet you think that you take responsibility in life because you take care of all the things that you agree to. Now let me ask you this.

- Are you happy with everything in your life?
- Is everything in your life going exactly the way you want it to?
- Your job?
- Your relationships?
- Where you live?
- The amount of money in your bank account?
- Your car?"

I'm gonna ask that same question of you after I share my response.

No!

I was not happy with everything in my life. Everything was not going exactly how I thought it should be or how I preferred it to be. I had come a long way since my divorce, but I couldn't look at my life and say everything was just the way I hoped for.

What does that have to do with responsibility? That's just the way life is.

"You are responsible for everything that is and everything that is not in your life. If it exists in your life, you created it through your thoughts, choices, and actions. If it's not there, you have created that as well," he said.

This is where I would insert a head explosion emoji if that sort of thing was currently acceptable in the world of book publication. This hit me like a bat to the head!

How could I have not seen the full picture before? It was so simple and so elusive all at the same time. This is what I mean when I say the words "radical responsibility." This simple perception shift changed my life.

That's it! I will do my best to no longer be the victim of my circumstances. No more.

This truth gave me the power to get back on the path toward my highest good. It is simple, magical and ruthless all at the same time, and it is merely a shift of perspective.

THE CAVEAT

I'm not saying it's going to be easy to do the work to create your beautiful story for yourself and manifest your dream of heaven here in this lifetime. However, I will assure you with every ounce of my being, if you're willing to commit, it will be worth every bit of effort!

Take a minute to consider your current situation. Is everything in your life going exactly how you would prefer, and would you change anything, if you had the option? Consider the questions listed above plus:

How do you feel when you see yourself in the mirror?

Are there any other parts of your life that come to mind? Are they causing you stress, just kind of blah, or amazingly wonderful?

Here is the flip side to being responsible for the good things—the shadow side. All of those issues and situations you'd change were manifested by you and your actions, or lack thereof.

You get all the credit for both the good and the bad, the positive and negative, the light and the shadow of your story.

This can be quite a kick to the gut as you examine the story of your life so far. When you choose to face the truth that you are responsible for everything, and I mean **everything,** there is nowhere else to point the finger. You may not have chosen the situation you were born into and maybe you didn't create your current situation with intention, but only you are responsible for how you respond moving forward and how you choose to walk in your world.

Ask yourself:

Will I continue to allow my old habits and patterns to guide my journey and create my story for me, or do I commit to doing the work to create new habits that will serve to lift me up higher and higher until my story doesn't even resemble the hell I have been accustomed to wallowing in?

STEP 1: AWARENESS

You must first become aware before you can make a change.

You are co-creating your story with life itself. Take back your power!

You are responsible for how you feel on the inside and how you show up on the outside.

- You are the dreamer of your dream, and only you can make it a beautiful dream of heaven or a terrible dream of hell.
- You choose whether to be the hero or the victim in your story.
- You, and only you, hold the power to choose a new path.

STEP 2: COMMITMENT

The work begins when you commit to saying "No" to your current story.

You are no longer going to accept this old way of letting your subconscious beliefs drive your perceptions and interpretations.

You're going to take back your power. You're going to take radical responsibility for yourself and the story of your life.

When you observe yourself having one of these reactions, you're going to stalk your thoughts—follow the line of thinking back to the root cause.

- What perception and interpretation have led me to this reaction?
- Does this perception serve me, or is there a different perception that would serve me at a higher level and work to quit giving my personal power away in this situation?

Not making a choice is a choice. Allowing unacceptable behaviors and situations is the same as choosing them.

STEP 3: PERCEPTION

Our beliefs shape our perceptions, our perceptions shape our interpretations, and these interpretations shape our reality.

This is the reason that two people can hear the same words and walk away with two different messages.

Once you're aware of how beliefs and perceptions shape your entire world, then you can start choosing your perceptions with conscious awareness.

You can shift your perception, which will create interpretations that'll serve your highest good and elevate your life to that which you have only imagined.

For example:

Someone cuts you off in traffic. What is your first reaction (notice I use the word reaction)?

Do you get angry, cuss them out, flip them off, honk your horn, or make sure they know just how unimpressed you are by their shitty driving in some other manner?

I know what you're thinking. *Of course, that is how I'm going to react. That A-hole just cut me off. They deserve to get a piece of my mind.*

These are reactions. These are subconscious responses to a predetermined perception of anyone who would drive "that way."

I get it. I have said many very unkind things to strangers who would never hear my words.

How does this leave you feeling? If you're like most people, this situation leaves you in some state of fight or flight. Does it somehow punish someone else for you to feel this way? Does being tense and angry serve you in some way or get you closer to your story of heaven?

Do you walk around in your day and randomly choose to get upset and angry? Of course not, so why would you choose to feel like that just because someone pulled in front of you in traffic in a manner that you thought was too close?

You're giving your power away to that person by choosing to let their behavior determine your inner state of being and write your story for you.

Perception is reality. New perceptions. New reality.

STEP 4: CHANGING YOUR PERCEPTION

You're going to create *seven* different perceptions about the situation that better serve to retain your power and create a more beautiful story.

Not more, not less. Seven, because it's enough to require you to stretch your brain without making the practice overly difficult.

Our first perception is usually driven by an assumption, which we proceed to take personally and react.

Let's use our getting cut off in traffic scenario, for example.

"They saw me and cut me off because they are a jerk," might be your first reaction. Plus, some pretty four-letter words, perhaps.

Now for seven different perceptions.

- He didn't see me in his blind spot and just changed lanes.
- She was preoccupied with her thoughts and didn't notice me.
- He may be rushing to the hospital to see a loved one who had an accident.
- She may have been talking to someone and not paying attention.
- He might be a new driver who is still trying to figure this out.
- What if that driver was my mother, brother, or daughter?
- How would I hope someone else would perceive me if I did the same thing?

With this list of seven new perceptions, you can now choose the one that serves to create a better story. Pick the one that most aligns with the beautiful story you are creating.

Remember, love and peace are our baselines. This is how we are designed.

STEP 5: LET THE OTHER SHIT GO

Now let's talk about what you're not responsible for. This is a simple list.

You're not responsible for anyone else's story, for anyone else's dream, or anyone else's life. They are the creators of their dream. They are the creators of their stories. They get to choose. They are radically responsible for themselves.

You are *not* responsible for helping, but you can *choose* to help when asked. You cannot make someone create a different story. It's not your place.

Become the master of your own story and watch the magic that grows in your wake. Allow others to create their own story just like you want them to allow you to create yours.

Now that you're aware of radical responsibility, you need not ever be the victim of your circumstances. You have the awareness and tools to choose.

Although situations will happen around you, you get to choose how you perceive them and respond. You get to choose what it means in your world. You always have a choice and you're responsible for that choice.

If you work towards the most loving and peaceful outcome, you'll find, without exception, a life that increases with love, joy, and peace internally and externally.

Let go of judgment. It is not our place to judge others, but more importantly, *quit judging yourself!*

Be authentically you. If you can dream it, you can achieve it. If it's your natural way of showing up, do it with gusto.

Be the creator of your heaven inside and out.

Love yourself unconditionally!

You are the love of your life.

You are the only person who's been there through everything in your life.

Be kind to yourself as you take responsibility for the way you've been treating yourself.

Make the changes that will create your most amazing story.

May you always see the perfect being that you are!

All my love!

Seth has spent countless hours in his pursuit of love and happiness. His spiritual journey is one of heart, his mission is to help people shift their awareness and level of consciousness, so they can transform their lives and step into their unique gifts and cosmic power.

Seth has served 17 years on the front line of the fire service. He is currently a fire captain in Washington State and a Swift Water Rescue instructor servicing surrounding fire departments.

He's a leadership coach, firefighter, emergency medical technician, Swift Water Rescue instructor, Reiki Master, Toltec Shaman with teachings from Jim Fortin, Don Juan lineage, and the Ruiz family, Eagle Knight Lineage.

Join me on social media and check out my website to see how I can be of service to you in further creating your beautiful story of life.

Connect with Seth

Instagram: Instagram.com/iamsethrohrer

Facebook: facebook.com/iamsethrohrer

Website: rohrerrevolution.com

"Perspective is everything - your life literally depends on it."

~ Seth Rohrer

Chapter 7

CHOOSING HOPE

NAVIGATING HARDSHIP WITH JOY AND GRACE

Justin Krull, PT

MY STORY

It was recess. The din of a thousand children playing and exploring filled my ears as I hurtled myself between and around other children standing around talking or playing more idly. I was hunting. Hot from the pursuit, my eight-year-old body loved the familiar burn in my chest and in my legs from a good old-fashioned game of tag. Suddenly, an unfamiliar pressure came across my chest and back. Then a stumbling underfoot. I was falling. No wait, *Was I just tackled?!*

I felt the wind get knocked out of my chest as I made contact with the hardened dirt. The pressure of another child laid into my back trapping me prone, and before I could gasp for air, suddenly an arm was wrapped around my throat. I attempted to thrash away, but my captor was strong, I was caught by surprise, and I couldn't breathe. I began to panic as I heard the boy growl as he excitedly squeezed harder. I tried to yell for help but could barely make a sound. Some of the surrounding children stopped what they were doing and watched, but nobody made a move—silent witnesses as I realized the child's pressure was intentionally on my windpipe. He really intended to hurt me. I pushed into the earth feebly with my hands, head and neck arched backward, gasping for any available air I could get. *I was dying.*

"Wait here," we were instructed. My assailant, who I still couldn't make out the features of through my flowing tears, sat just two chairs away from me. I felt a shiver spread through my body as we sat in the large grey office lobby, quiet and alone. Surrounded by windows, it was like sitting in a fishbowl and the last thing I wanted right now was to be seen. Finally, the vice principal arrived, and we were interrogated. "What happened? Who started it?" She began. Her tone was assertive and aggressive. I sat in disbelief as the boy started, attempting to defend his position. *Wait, wait, wait; We were **both** sent to the principal's office. Does she honestly think that I might have started this? That this was somehow **my fault?** I am a good kid; I listen in class, and I do well; I respect the golden rule.*

A sense of disconnected numbness overtook me once more as my thoughts turned to unrecognizable gibberish and my body clamped up tightly waiting for the assault to finally end.

It wasn't until much later that I recognized the strange and juxtaposing relationship with attention and success this event created in my life. I was always taught the importance and value of academic achievement and service to my community, and I derived a great sense of joy from chasing it. Yet every time I was acknowledged for my efforts, criticized or corrected gently for my mistakes or shortcomings, or teased, I was flushed and red, sweaty, and nervous. Sometimes I'd even involuntarily tear up or cry, and I'd almost always feel a light constriction around my neck. Every time I was acknowledged, I was seen, and being seen made me vulnerable to attack, and my fight-flight response was thoroughly activated. Thankfully, I valued my success over honoring my anxiety, and over time, I leaned into challenging things. It didn't matter if the arm I held my student council election speech in was shaking involuntarily (like it was possessed) in front of 1500 of my peers as long as I secured the position. Ignoring and denying my physiology was totally fine. That would never come to haunt me later, right? *Right?*

Well, as you can guess, that strategy eventually failed during my training as a physical therapist. It turns out the strain of maintaining academic excellence in a condensed 24-month masters program filled with other stressed out, high achieving, type-A students, while trying to maintain a healthy relationship with my now wife, while planning a wedding, was just a little too much.

Oxygen felt like it was constantly coming at a premium—with every breath a shallow, unsatisfying sigh. When challenged, I felt that familiar tension in my throat and my thoughts spiraled into a scrambled mess. We struggled to communicate. Suddenly I was incredibly sensitive, not just to *what* I was feeling criticized for, but to *how* that criticism was delivered by my instructors. My wife and I had big plans for our careers, having mused openly about someday owning our own practice together. But by the time we came home from completing our national licensing exam, we both collapsed in the living room, having survived a two-year barrage of emotional damage, utterly spent. As I jumped from clinic to clinic, I constantly looked to my employers for the professional recognition and financial stability I thought would validate my career choices and make me feel safe and whole so I could finally breathe. I gave any power I had over my situation away.

Everything changed for me during my first Myofascial Release course. I found myself standing there in the hotel banquet hall, surrounded by my peers, and yet utterly alone. I was choking and unable to speak. Nothing else mattered as I struggled for breath. As I stood there in the flow of deep tribal drums, our instructor, John Barnes's voice beckoned us to breathe in and out deeper and deeper. Finally, at the apex, he asked us to start vocalizing the strongest yell from the deepest depths of our bodies that we could muster, and I began to scream.

I screamed for eternity. I screamed until there was nothing left. I screamed as I threw that kid off me with the strength of a savage beast. I screamed until there was no more room for the fear in this memory to live in my body any longer. And then finally I wept; I shook; I convulsed; I was leaking from my face.

"What is a healthier way to think, feel, and act now?" John asked. At first no answer came, just a slowly building sense of peace as I rocked back and forth gently and held myself. It was about 30 minutes of this until the experience was over and I felt like myself again, only lighter somehow. I stretched as my face opened into a huge, deeply satisfying yawn. I was teary but giggling as joy seeped into my face in the form of a warm smile.

The event had shocked my system, clearing away the physiology of my trauma so I could see what it had wrought and finally *choose* how to move forward. I hadn't realized until that day that a small part of me, somewhere deep in the recesses of my body, was stuck, struggling for life, all this time.

What do I want? I pondered. *What matters to me most? Why?*

I give myself permission to live, and enjoy my life.

I choose hope.

My eight-year-old self lacked the context that growing into adulthood and developing self-reflective skills provides. He scrambled to understand and find meaning from what happened that day so long ago and crafted a subconscious message around what is required for me to feel safe. This *story* is written at the moment of impact for all of our physical and emotional traumas. No damage has or ever will be inflicted upon you without an emotional context, and the stories we tell about it, however flawed or skewed, become our lived truth.

This is where I will piss you off a little bit and rattle your cage. I want you to know that I say this with the utmost love and care and respect for you and your experiences, which I may never have objectively experienced myself.

The problem is that your story about what happened to you, while you're still living it, has no therapeutic value.

It was written through the lens of the very trauma or hardship you're struggling to overcome. The story shackles you to the trauma. It doesn't hold up to scrutiny once the underlying flawed subconscious message has been discovered, because that underlying message is almost always rooted in fear. It's not about what happened; it's about the perception of the events and the emotional weight that holds. This is why I, like many of us, waltzed through life repeating the same maladaptive patterns over and over.

I've learned that changing your mind is a matter of persistently challenging your perceptions and subconscious beliefs. Words matter, and can easily be wielded as a sword for self-punishment or a shield for self-reflection. Breaking your thought patterns allows you to observe your story from outside of its lived experience and begin feeling your way through. We need that shock to get out of our own way. Once you begin to see the flaws in your own logic, you open the door for change in your life to occur.

"Okay, so before we start our objective assessment, I have one final question for you: What is your goal for our time together?"

I could barely keep my composure as the "I've got a secret to share" grin strained to break through. She shifted uneasily in the cozy teal chair. She didn't realize it yet, but like a puzzle fresh from the box, pieces strewn chaotically across the table, her symptoms, traumas, and *story* were laid bare, and everything she needed to heal was now right there.

Now tell me what you really want. Tell me your hopes and dreams! I'm ready.

Expectedly, she repeated from her intake form: "I want to feel less pain. I want to be able to walk more without getting sore."

"Okay, and that is a perfectly reasonable goal, but it's boring." I grin cheekily. "Those are my functional goals for you as a physiotherapist." I use air quotes changing the intonation of my voice as I say, "Improve subjective pain rating from eight to zero out of ten. Increase walking tolerance by 20 minutes."

I put my arms down, speaking normally as I continued, "They are achievable, but they have no real value to you." I see her head cock to the side as she stares back at me in confusion.

"If I snapped my fingers and suddenly everything you described that was bothering you was gone, what would you do? What do you want to feel when you wake up in the morning, when you engage with your partner or your kids? What would not having pain give you? Why do you care about walking more?"

I challenge patients with questions like these because while objective therapeutic goals are important, they often aren't strong enough to support the creation of a consistent self-care or mindfulness-based practice that will carry patients through to living their best life. Homework doesn't feel like homework if you care deeply about its practice. Healing is more than a list of problems to be solved. It's about creating a vision for yourself greater than your current circumstances informed by what really matters to you. It's about cultivating a "why" that keeps you going even when things get hard, or the motivation is gone.

THE PRACTICE

Perhaps you have also created SMART (Specific, Measurable, Attainable, Realistic, and Timely) goals for your health and healing and are at a loss as to why it seems nigh impossible to achieve some of them. Grab a piece of paper and your favorite pen and follow along with these five questions as we transform your SMART goals into a vision you can get behind.

QUESTION 1: WHAT IS YOUR STORY?

Our lives are full of experiences, memories, and emotions. Like snapshots in time, they create the tapestry of our lives. These stories help us interpret a sense of meaning, purpose, and value. Sometimes our subconscious just needs to feel like it's been heard. Set a timer for five minutes and write out your story. Focus particularly on the things that you currently wish you had some control over or could change. This is your opportunity to voice your chief complaint.

QUESTION 2: WHAT IS YOUR STORY *REALLY?*

There are typically three voices rattling around in your head. The intuitive voice tends to speak kindly to and about you. When you are centered, it almost feels like the universe is co-creating with you through this voice, cheering you on. Your own internal voice is when you hear yourself ask a question or narrate what you're doing, or you're reading this book! The final voice is the pessimistic voice that likes to shit all over your happiness and self-esteem.

For some of us, that's the voice that speaks first or the loudest, reinforcing and trapping us in trauma. The ironic part is that none of these three voices are actually *you.* Our brains communicate in *visuals and pictures* with an estimated processing power of ten million to one versus our intellectual intelligence. We *learn* the language to communicate our ideas to others. It's a tool we can all too easily wield against ourselves like a club. Our intuition knows when it's being hosed, and it leaves marks in the form of emotions and patterns in thinking and behavior and sometimes movement. Changing your goals and your mindset requires stepping back and seeing your hardship from the perspective of an observer of these three voices.

Let's take five more minutes now and look at your page from the previous activity. Go through it line by line and without judgment ask yourself the question, "Is it true?" Wait for a response from your mind, and then wait a little longer. Observe if the pessimist's voice chimes in and how quickly. Was it first? Did you have a calm, objective answer come and then have it interrupted? Also, notice your physiology. Did anything you wrote make you feel gross, or create tension in your body? Did your heart rate or breath change? Most importantly, as you go through your list, regardless of which voices seem to visit you, notice what on your page still stands up to objective scrutiny and what falls away as being false. Once five minutes are up scribble down the first thing that comes to mind as being the actual story, the truth, the true root cause of your current hardship that requires addressing.

QUESTION 3: WHAT DO YOU WANT?

Now that you've observed what is actually true, you get to decide what you actually want to feel or change or achieve. Go ahead and dream big. Don't overthink it. Quickly now, in one or two sentences describe what you picked this book up to change in the first place and write it down.

QUESTION 4: WHAT DO YOU *REALLY* WANT?

I don't even know what you've written on your page, but I can almost guarantee that you're dreaming too small. Most people I ask this question to use "more" or "less" statements when describing what they want. More or less than what? There is no power there. As a PT, I can help get you one percent better and you'll technically feel more mobile and less sore. Is that good enough? Of course not. I *dare* you to dream bigger.

For example, instead of "I want to feel more connected with my body," try "I want to feel connected with my body." Stop self-limiting! For this next step set a timer for five minutes and close your eyes. Imagine your life if what you wanted to feel or achieve was already yours. What would that look, feel, smell, sound, and taste like? How did you dream before you got hurt? This is the magic sauce that puts your body into a higher physiological state and makes transformation possible. If you can feel it like it's already yours then nothing can stop you. When you're done, open your eyes and write me a big hairy audacious, outrageous but achievable, exciting, delicious goal for what you want to have or feel in your life once that hardship is no more.

QUESTION 5: WHY DOES IT MATTER TO YOU?

Finally, we must anchor your amazing new vision for your future to the things you care about that will act as your fuel. These are the unwavering *key values* that will carry you through even when motivation starts to slip. In the journey to create a habit-changing mindset, stagnation is like poison to your big, beautiful dream. Knowing what your achievement will provide you, if it's important enough, will always keep you motivated. A sense of peace and self-connection? Purpose? Vitality? Do you want to feel autonomy over your own life? Do you want to feel the buzz of being social once more? Do you want to feel present and available for your kids? The *what* is the vision for the joy already yours, while the *why* is the mantra that supports it, rooted in patience and grace.

Be sure to question *who* you're changing for. Big hint to all those martyrs and empaths: The first person on that list must be you since you can't fill anyone else's cup if yours has a massive hole in it. The others on that list should also be your biggest supporters and cheerleaders. Use their support as much as you possibly can. Anybody who really cares about you should be rooting for your success but remember that you need to root for yourself first to show them how because chances are good that they've never dreamed this big for themselves before either.

Now finish strong by writing out your why.

Remember that if you have the occasional setback, or it feels impossibly hard at first as you start down your healing path, it's okay, because feeling is healing, the only way out is through, and with a keen focus on who you are becoming and why it matters, you are building a life greater than any hardship, trauma, or pain you might experience.

You are powerful beyond measure.

You can do this.

Choose hope.

 **Justin Krull,** PT, is co-owner of Myofascial Release Mississauga, where he regularly helps clients make massive changes in their minds and bodies so they can realize their greatest healing potential. He has been practicing Myofascial Release, a hands-on manual therapy that addresses the integrated mind-body connection, since graduating with a Master of Science in Physical Therapy from the University of Toronto in 2011. Through thorough postural evaluation and assessment, the skilled application of sustained pressures, mindful movement practices, and supplemental therapies, the award-winning clinic he helps manage with his wife and business partner has become a community hub for people suffering from chronic pain to find hope and healing.

His ongoing mission is to achieve the future of chronic pain management in his local, global, spiritual, and professional communities through Myofascial Release and mindful movement practices so that every person touched by his practice may learn and grow as patients, professionals, and human beings. By doing this he dreams that every person may learn to find, recognize, and foster hope from within themselves and ultimately experience the joy that comes from living a lifestyle greater than their pain and rich in abundance.

When Justin is relaxing, you'll find him jogging to his favorite music, painting or collecting for a variety of nerdy hobbies, playing with his two wonderful children outdoors, or enjoying a delicious vegetarian meal with the love of his life at a local restaurant.

Connect with Justin:

Website: https://www.myofascialmississauga.com

Facebook: https://www.facebook.com/myofascialmississauga

Instagram: https://www.instagram.com/myofascialmississauga

TikTok: http://www.tiktok.com/@myofascialmississauga

Free Facebook Community for self-care resources, Fascial Freedom: https://www.facebook.com/groups/fascialfreedom

"Healing is more than a list of problems to be solved. It's about creating a vision for yourself greater than your current circumstances informed by what really matters to you. It's about cultivating a why rooted in patience and grace that keeps you going even when things get hard, or the motivation is gone."

~ Justin Krull

Chapter 8

GOOD MINDSET = GOOD LIFE!

LETTING GO OF CONTROL FOR ULTIMATE FREEDOM

Sharon Josef, Ph.D, Channeler, Medical Intuitive

MY STORY

I asked my guides about the topic of mindset as it relates to me, and they said: "Why do you try to control the loss of control?" Initially, I had no idea what this meant. I saw myself as the last person who would try to control anyone or anything. I always let people choose for themselves what they want to do with their lives and how they want to do it. As far as controlling the situation, I thought I always accept *what is* and flow with it.

However, upon further analysis, I realized that my guides were referring to my childhood, specifically as it concerns my maternal grandmother, who lived with us. My mother always tried to please her mother. No matter what my grandmother asked for, my mother listened and obeyed. There was peace as long as my grandmother felt in control of the house. My grandmother started an argument whenever my father asked my mother (his wife) for something that made her less available to her mother. Many times my grandma would say to my mom: "I need my hair done" (meaning by my mom), or "Go get these items from the store; I need them now," or "What is he-she saying on TV?" (while interrupting the show for whoever was present). My mom would drop whatever she was doing and take care of her mom. My granny also insisted that my mom go out with her to visit other members of the extended family; even though my dad did not want to go out with her, my mom obeyed my granny.

This dynamic obviously impacted me as a child. Being a strong-minded individual, I responded by intervening on behalf of my father. I raised my voice in defense of my father in front of my mother and grandmother: "Why don't you let her be with Dad. Stop ordering her around and asking her to do things that take her away from Dad." This was my way of taking back control. I felt bad for my father for not having the freedom to have the relationship he deserved with his wife.

This was the first time I tried to "control the loss of control." The truth was that my father could have stepped up and asked my mother to change things, or he could've even asked my grandmother to leave. But instead, he just let things be how they were and never said anything (that I'm aware of). That was his choice and his journey to make.

The next time I tried to "control the loss of control" was in my late teens. My brother asked to take a trip to Canada on his last vacation from the army. When he got back, he announced to my parents: "I am moving to Canada. Would you follow me?" My parents talked among themselves and then asked me: "Would you like us to follow Adrian and move to Canada?" As I adored my brother, I agreed without thinking twice. "Of course I will!"

In Canada, my father planned to start a business using a new machine he invented. The machine was used to harden metals, which could be extremely helpful in the industrial field. Companies using machines to build everything from bottle caps to car parts used machinery in the production process. Over time, the production machines suffered from wear and tear, so a process to make the metal pieces in those machines stronger was valuable.

As planned, my father started a company, gave my brother a part of it, and took on another investor to handle the logistics. My brother and the partner ended up going behind my father's back and putting the patent for the machine in my brother's name only. My brother proceeded to start a few companies using my father's machine. As for my father, each time he created a new company, the partners tried to steal his machine (especially after speaking to my brother).

My brother kept coming over and asking my dad to do things differently: "You are thinking too small," he'd say to my dad. "We should do things on a bigger scale, going to each company and getting one client at a time is a waste of time. Let's get a team of many salesmen to go all over Canada, the United States, and Europe all at once." The arguing back and forth caused a lot of suffering for a long time. It's hard for me to write this, but it even got to the point that my brother said to my uncle: "I am sure I was switched at birth. It cannot be that he is my father." The general feeling in the house was pretty grim. My grandmother, who was very connected to my brother, always tried to mend things and pushed my mother to intervene with my father on my brother's behalf. I felt very protective of my father and was mad at my brother for hurting my parents and for disappointing me. I really adored him and had always looked up to him up to this point. By the time I turned 21, my father had been diagnosed with cancer. It took about a year for him to transition to the other side. As you can imagine, I was devastated.

To make matters worse, in the last few weeks before my father's death, my mother gave my brother a kidney (he lost both kidneys earlier and was on dialysis for a few years). My mother and brother were in one hospital, while my father was in another. I was taking care of my father until he went into the hospital. I drove him to chemo and always tried to make him laugh. I put my life on hold while my dad was sick. At 20, I didn't care to go out and have fun like any 20-year-old. I kept praying: *Please don't die; I will do whatever it takes to keep him here comfortable and happy as long as I can.* At the hospital, I sat by his bedside feeling very sad and helpless: *what can I offer or what promise can I make that will keep my dad here?* I had this big hole and heaviness in my heart. It felt like the ground was pulled from under me. *I don't want to keep living in this pain.* At home, my father's family flew in from Brazil to be by his side, and my grandmother fought with them constantly. My father's partners were trying to take over the company at work. In other words: there was a total loss of control all around me.

While he was in the hospital, my father said to me: "Go to the office, take the machine I built and use it for yourself," with the hope I'd be able to use it one day to support myself and the family. I replied, "Okay, Dad, don't worry about this now." The night before he died, I managed to safely take the machine home (and out of the hands of his scheming partners). The pain around this machine was so great that I put it in a box, never to be found again. It took me 30 years to realize that when I put the machine in a box, I also put part of myself in that box—the part that loved and trusted people and was ready to take on life with all of my power.

It took me way too long to learn how to not try to control the uncontrollable. I still catch myself from time to time trying to control situations, and in those moments, I need to remind myself not to fall into old ways of thinking.

The solution to stop the default reaction of old mindsets (or the way to change your mindset) is to *let joy guide you.*

By focusing on joy (or dreams you have), you can transform your beliefs quicker than if you try to transform your beliefs by having to go through heartache and spiraling lessons. When you're focused on something that matters to you greatly or that you want to create or establish in your life, you let go of old beliefs and do things regardless of your fears.

What I wrote in this last paragraph is the ideal situation. Hopefully, change can occur this way in our life, where dreams and desires lead the way. Thinking back to my desires in the past, when I wanted to move to the states, it didn't enter my mind that I needed a green card to be able to work here. At 25, I made my mother promise that she would follow me and send some of my prize possessions, like my spiritual books, etc. I hopped on a plane and came to Los Angeles. The idea was to work with my brother, who would sponsor me to get my green card.

Things didn't go as I had planned, and I needed to get a job. When I applied for a job, they asked me if I had a green card or permission to work there. "It's in progress," I said. At the time, it was not in progress yet, but it was about to be. I thought I'd also get a programming job in a different company (I have a computer science degree), and at the time, companies were looking for programmers. I was offered a job by a company that offered to get me my green card, and that's how I eventually got it. But, back to the current position I was being interviewed for, the employer sent me to an office with a lie detector machine to ensure the green card was in progress. At the time, the government was rightfully penalizing any company that didn't hire employees legally able to work in the states. From the interview to the office for the lie detection test, I kept reciting to my subconscious mind that it was (the green card) being worked on, convincing my subconscious and my body not to react differently when I was asked that question. I have no idea how I knew to do that!

I'm happy to report that I passed the test. My body did not react differently when I was asked the question: "Are you legally allowed to work in the states?" My body and I were calm and cool as a cucumber. I'm sure each of you reading this has a story of wanting something so badly you walked through fire to get it. Think back. What was it for you?

In the story above, I had to upgrade or tweak my belief or reach for a belief that was new to me: *If I repeat to myself that I am eligible to work here, I can get what I desire.*

My newest dream is to open a healing or retreat center. I've wanted this for a long time but was never ready to focus on making it a reality. The dream is to have it out in nature, surrounded by trees and wildlife. I shared my dream when I met my husband some 30 years ago. "Will you join me and help me create this?" At the time, my husband said yes. Our focus changed as the years went by, and we grew a family. As I became more spiritual, my husband was less into it, so he told me he no longer had a desire to be part of that dream of mine. Recently I presented the healing center as a business to him. "I realize that even though I have the intention for this center to help people become more spiritually aware, I'm going to consider that it's a business. I want it to thrive." What I said sparked his interest. "I might join you," he said.

The understanding I gained recently, with the help of the guides, was that I'm always making sure everyone is in harmony, not only within themselves but also in their home and relationships. I've been quieting my real opinion and truth for so long. All I focus on is not to ruffle anyone's feathers in any way, not allow chaos to exist for others, and make sure to advise and act in harmony. Hence my voice, knowledge, and energy are all stuffed inside. No wonder I always felt overwhelmed. That's why I'm looking for great, large spaces (for the retreat- healing center) in nature and travel so I can feel the spaciousness I need inside!

Now I will be making a jump in mindset. To step into my full power (not from an ego standpoint), be in my truth, and still make my dreams come true, I want to start exercising my voice louder. I want to no longer be in fear if someone doesn't feel good about what I say or what there is for them in their experience. I no longer want to take on the responsibility of caring for anyone who comes into my experience. I want to detach from any outcome my clients experience due to my healing. Not that I don't care. I care very much! But as my guides recommended years ago, I want to ensure I have detached compassion. As we open up our mindset further, we receive more and more information on how to make our life better and easier.

When it comes to mindset, it encompasses everything in our life. First, I feel we need to deal with the issues that keep coming up. Then we need to focus on welcoming abundance on all levels and in all ways. We usually have to change our belief system (or mindset) when it comes to money, but also love, relationships, and careers.

It's the way we allow love in that allows us to be and feel abundant. It's mostly, and firstly, self-love that matters, and that is where most of us fall short. Yes, we can say from our head: *I truly love myself unconditionally,* but it's a different matter to own it in our bodies and in how we conduct ourselves in our lives. You can quickly tell how you feel about yourself when you follow the tools below.

THE PRACTICE

The following are facts that I always have in the back of my mind. They helped me create the freedom of choice in anything in my life. I also make sure to remind my clients of these facts; they create an important way of looking at and living in this world. They are all understandings I got through the stories above. I do believe these complement the work of loving yourself deeper.

The list below contains five universal truths. Keep these in mind rather than the old rules you may have acquired from religious lessons, miseducation, simple ignorance of friends or caregivers, or beliefs we formed from our life experiences which we may have translated poorly. Keeping these in mind will enable you to look at life from an easier perspective.

One: Energy is generally neutral. It's what you make of it. We tell ourselves far too many stories that we don't need to. We can feel sad without needing to have a reason behind it. There is no bad energy unless your vibrations are low. If you spend your thoughts on being sad, down, jealous, unsatisfied, disappointed, etc., your vibrations will be low, and you'll attract whatever vibrates at that rate. It's the same as saying if you're afraid of something and you keep thinking about it, that is exactly what will take place because all of our energy is focused there. The question is, what would you like to create? Focus on the end result of what you would like, and work it backward.

Two: There are no victims, only a victim mentality. On some level (soul, higher-self level), even the bad things that took place in our lives (our traumas) are known to us before we incarnate. We still choose them to balance our karma, learn necessary lessons, or overcome other experiences, like those from our past lives. Please forgive me if you've been through unimaginable abuse or the loss of a child, or other devastating experience. I don't mean to belittle your experience at all! I also know you wouldn't have chosen to take this particular journey if you could not manage it. By having to get over such experiences, one comes into their power, and many times one also comes to the understanding of their contribution. We all contribute to the collective. We are all part of the one. You could call it creation if you prefer.

Three: By being part of God-Goddess-All-That-Is, we're part of the divine spark. As such, we can **create.** And we do, just with our thoughts. We are creator beings. When something we desire does not come about, it's because we let fear get in the way or we don't persist in what we desire (i.e., we lose interest). I'm not speaking of desiring someone. We each have free will! We cannot make someone do or feel what we want them to; that is manipulation. Also, being the spark of all that is makes us **worthy** just by being-existing. We spend a great part of our life looking for our worth through the eyes of our loved ones, friends, co-workers, achievements, etc., when, in fact, we're worthy from our birth. We don't need to make a lot of money to be worthy, nor do we need to have an amazing career or make amazing contributions to humanity (although that's a bonus) to be worthy. Imagine if each of us truly loved ourselves completely and unconditionally. Then imagine how full our cup would feel; it would runneth over. And now, imagine if we had so much self-love, wouldn't we want to give love to everyone around us? And then it would be collectively in each country and each continent, etc. Is that what could bring peace? And in fact, we couldn't have peace without changing our mindset to an understanding that we each want to do our own work and love ourselves deeply, so we can have the capacity to embody love on a collective basis.

Four: There is no "should" or "have to," nor is there a God that tells us what to do. We are each our own God from a soul perspective. We decide for ourselves what we want to work on or heal in this life or on this journey. Also, contracts can be undone. Our compass is our joy.

Five: Lastly, for now, there is an unlimited amount of resources in this universe. Start thinking big for yourself and for our world. There are alternative energies we have not explored yet. As for you personally, don't be afraid to think outside the box. Reach out for support and ideas. They are always available.

MASTERY TOOL—MIRROR WORK

This may sound like a known process, but my guides take us deeper. It is The Mirror work:

1. Look into your eyes in the mirror and say: "I love you."

    All the bells and whistles and the shitty committee saboteur's voice will come in loud and clear. Whatever it says against yourself, your job is to respond: "I love you with _____(fill in the blank). For example, your mind may tell you your thighs are too big, so you respond: "I love you with your big thighs." Or, "I love you with your stupidity," or whatever other negative trait you tell yourself. No matter what your negative inner voice says, your job is to tell yourself you love yourself with whatever it is.

2. Say it as many times a day as possible. You do not need to be in front of the mirror. Our subconscious takes in what we say or think at face value. It does not question: Is this statement true? Does she-he really mean it?

3. Say it for at least 60 days. Thirty days will create a new neural pathway in your brain, but 60 days will make sure that you establish a strong neural pathway. Remember that we operate 95-96% of the time from our subconscious mind. So if we create this strong new pathway, it will operate from there.

Remember that your outer reality is a reflection of your inner one. Hence, when we love ourselves more deeply, it's like looking through pink glasses—everything looks better, and everyone in your life also sees you with colored glasses. So enjoy deepening your self-love and changing your mindset. It will make your life so much easier and enjoyable.

With so much gratitude and love.

Sharon Joseph has professionally coached people in their personal growth for close to 20 years. She is a channeler, a healer, a bestselling author, a medium, an animal communicator, a DNA architect, and a clairvoyant.

Sharon is a mirror for others to explore and embrace who they are, supporting them as they step into the fullness of their being. Using her astute medical intuition (X-ray vision), she can interpret the language of the body when it comes to ailments and or energetic blocks. She gives down-to-earth tools on how to release these blocks and uses her fast and powerful healing ability to assist in healing. She also uses her clairvoyance, energy interpretation, and her gift as a medium to help one upgrade their awareness and their life. Sharon helps people uncover and focus on what they can accomplish in any area of life, including personal growth, health, love, relationships, success, and career.

Sharon achieved a Bachelor's degree in computer science with a minor in business as well as a Ph.D. in Metaphysical Science. She is an ordained minister. As a citizen of the world, Sharon respects all paths to the One. Her passions include animals, laughing, dancing, travel, meditation, and connecting with like-minded people.

She is currently guiding people to release their old stories on all levels and step into their joy. She does it through one-on-one sessions and classes (online and in person), and she also conducts retreats worldwide.

Connect with Sharon:

Website: www.sharonjosef.com

Email: sharonjosef8@gmail.com

Facebook: https://www.facebook.com/SharonNitka/

Instagram: https://www.instagram.com/sharonjo/

Twitter: https://twitter.com/sharonJ84151501

LinkedIn: https://www.linkedin.com/in/sharon-josef-04896a7a/

"It's the way we allow love in
that allows us to be and feel abundant."

~ Sharon Josef

Chapter 9

THE MAGIC POWER OF YOUR MIND

HOW TO CHANGE YOUR LIFE, ONE THOUGHT AT A TIME

Rika Markel, Success and Mindset Coach, Clearing Facilitator

MY STORY

"Again?"

"You're going *again?*"

The emphasis was on the word "again."

The tone felt accusatory.

As if I was committing a crime.

A few years earlier, or even a few months earlier, that would have created a rush of anxiety in my body, a dry mouth, and physical unease, but at this point, I just felt peace.

I heard myself say: "Yes, I'm going again."

"When are you leaving?"

"October sixth or seventh, not really sure yet."

Then there was silence.

That was it; there was nothing more to say.

I had no intention of defending myself, nor was I going to change my mind.

My next trip was planned. I love road trips; they connect me with who I really am, no more hiding and feeling guilty about it.

The vibes I sent out were just peace and certainty, so the other party understood subconsciously that there was nothing to talk about.

That was it.

I was going *again.*

It was the end of an era.

Until today, my whole life was built around seeking freedom, a place where only happiness and bliss exist, a connection to something bigger, life the way it was supposed to be, life without pain and suffering—immortality.

Three marriages, five children, five grandchildren, different jobs, moving 38 times (really, not a joke), even to another continent, didn't do the work.

I could use so many one-liners here, but none would pinpoint what I really mean.

Bottom line: there is no seeking, there is nothing to look for, and there is nothing out there; it was here all the time.

The beginning of my new life. I picked up where I left off a few decades ago, but now, armed with so much more experience, knowledge, and above all, faith. An awareness which was so peaceful that the struggles leading me to this moment were worth it.

The pain and the darkness that created this path to knowing became insignificant.

For as long as I can remember, I knew my thoughts created my reality, that words have power, and that there is only one person responsible for my life, and that is me, myself, and I.

For that same reason, I had this twisted relationship with reality because why on earth would I create the results I had if I didn't like them?

There was a lot of good in my life but also a lot of pain, drama, and trauma.

Where did this come from?

About three years ago, my life went downhill fast. I didn't sleep because of the anxiety I felt, I was in constant physical pain, and it felt to me that despite the work I did on myself, things just worsened rapidly.

I was doing something wrong—big time.

Results never lie.

And my results were not inspiring.

Being a seeker my whole life, I did what I do best: I started seeking the reason for my discomfort; I needed to know what was going on. *What happened to me? How did I get here?*

I started reading even more books, followed courses, went on retreats and road trips, meditated daily, stopped drinking alcohol, and stopped taking pain meds. I took care of my body by seeing an acupuncturist and chiropractor, made an inventory of my thoughts, released blockages, taught myself self-hypnosis, and the list goes on.

My healing became a job and hard work.

I smile when I write these things down. What a list - so much work - but I was still beating myself up at the end of the day.

I was still thinking I could do more; I was still unhappy with the results, and I told myself I was close. I told myself: *if you keep doing this, the results will come.*

And then, one moment, not that long ago, I just *saw* it.

When I *think* I can do more, that's exactly what I get.

When I don't *feel* happy with the results, that's exactly what I get.

When I think results will come, that's exactly what will happen. They will come, implying that they are never here yet.

I stopped.

I started to do things without attachment.

Almost instantly, the whole dynamic changed. It was amazing how fast the results came.

Our thoughts *really* create our reality.

It's so simple; it's a universal law. It's amazing to me that we never learn how to use our minds so we *can* create a healthy and abundant life.

Our mind is the organ in our body that does just that—create our reality.

At this point in my life, I understand there is no way to explain how it really works. There's nothing to learn, nothing to understand; it just is.

Words are not enough to get to the bottom of what is really going on.

In what follows here, I will do my best to explain what it means for our thoughts to create our reality.

We are living on this planet, which is a 3D reality. We connect to the world with our senses. We see, feel, touch, hear, and smell.

Our senses create emotions and feelings stored in the mind as memories.

We all have those moments when we smell a certain smell, and immediately it reminds us of our grandparent's house or a childhood friend's house. This is how our mind is programmed. We store memories, which are used to create your experiences in this lifetime.

We can say then that our mind is an information bank, the same way that the software in your computer stores information, and results are generated when you know how to use the software.

That generating of information arises effortlessly.

You put in data; you want to run a list, one click of the button, and there it is, simple.

Same for your mind. You see something, your mind goes into the stored memory bank, and there arises a thought effortlessly.

The accumulation of those thoughts is creating your reality.

That's it.

It's not hard to understand then that most of our experiences are completely controlled by our memories.

I'm scared of cats because of an experience I had as a baby, so now, every time I see a cat, that feeling of fear comes up, and it unfolds in my life as terror; this happens automatically.

If I want to eliminate my fear of cats, I'll have to rewire my program, erase my memories, and create a new set of connections to have a different experience in the future.

Again, simple.

But there is more.

On top of this, we also know that we're not human beings that can have a spiritual experience; we are spiritual beings having an earthly experience.

There is this limitless awareness flowing to and through us.

That limitless awareness is who we really are.

This is what we mean when we say: We are one.

We are all connected.

We are all part of that limitless awareness, a spirit with no beginning and no end.

When you are really in touch with this concept, you know that these words don't do this awareness justice. This awareness is a deep knowing.

For this awareness to have an earthly experience, it can take many forms. It (the awareness) can be expressed, for example, as a rock, tree, animal, or human being.

Let me point out the word we use: human **being.**

We don't call ourselves human **doing**

because that wouldn't be correct, we are human **beings.**

We just are.

Our true nature is just **being.**

And here is the kicker:

The limitless awareness communicates with us (the body-mind) through the organ of the mind. At first, it's a knowing, what we'd call a gut feeling or urge, and then it translates to the body using thoughts.

The bottom line is that there are two kinds of thoughts: thoughts that come from our programs, and thoughts that come from our true nature.

We identify the "I" with our body because that's how we're programmed as little kids—most of us unlearn to listen to our gut.

How often did you do something you knew wasn't good for you, but you did it anyway because you wanted to conform?

How often do you do something because you reason this is the best thing for you, but the information is based on your programming and not on your gut feeling?

In order for us to be really happy and fulfilled, it's key to know who you really are.

You're a limitless being using a body so that you can experience a 3D life.

The key is to use our body-mind to our benefit and not to create fear, anxiety, and depression.

Understanding that everything will unfold effortlessly is the secret to abundance on all levels.

What religions would call putting your trust in God.

The only problem with this is that the commentators of the words of God, or what I would call the rules of the universe, didn't do such a good job explaining the real truth.

That's why those words create more separation than unity. We only have to look at history to know this is true.

In this time and age, more and more people wake up.

It's easier than ever before to recognize your true nature.

It's like the four-minute mile. Once one person did it, many others followed shortly thereafter because the belief changed.

I'm hopeful that more and more people will wake up to their true nature—knowing they are limitless, effortless beings.

When more people start to create their reality consciously, the whole dynamic of the planet will change.

Instead of fighting against poverty, let's focus on abundance for all.

Instead of fighting against global warming, let's focus on the perfect climate.

Instead of fighting against discrimination of all sorts, let's focus on equality.

Mother Teresa knew exactly what she was talking about when she said: "I was once asked why I don't participate in anti-war demonstrations. I said that I will never do that, but as soon as you have a pro-peace rally, I'll be there."

Whatever you focus on, you get more of. By changing your thoughts, you don't only change your reality, you change the reality of all.

I'm beyond grateful that I woke up and recognized my true nature.

I follow my gut; I allow my life to unfold effortlessly.

I listen to the urge in me to travel, to talk about my awakening without fear.

Yes, I am going. . .again.

Yes, I'm living my life of bliss in every moment.

And yes, I wish that you will find your bliss in every moment of the day.

THE PRACTICE

Being a seeker my whole life, I can now see how thinking there was something out there that I had to attach to was holding me back for many decades.

My body-mind developed at a very young age to think others were smarter and better than me. Listening to my feelings was tricky and the safe way of life was to conform.

Even though I knew deep inside that others were on the same path, not better, not smarter, but just different, I would've done everything to fit in.

It was that feeling—knowing that what was in front of me was not true—that kept me in the loop of the seeker and made me go out pursuing the truth.

I still have days when the urge to seek is very much alive, but I know better now.

There is nothing to find; it's all already in me.

There is nothing out there that's going to do the job.

Real bliss, happiness, and abundance are found in awareness.

As much as I can give you a tool that helped me realize my true nature, don't be disappointed if it's different for you.

TOOL 1: BECOMING AWARE OF YOUR TRUE NATURE

I invite you to take a good look at the following pointers.

Don't try to do them all at once.

I recommend leaving at least three to four days between them. Read the pointer you're working with that day repeatedly and contemplate what it means to you. Try to use all your senses while doing so. As much as our senses are 3D related, they are the primary tools to translate the language of who you really are.

- Think about how everything in nature unfolds without effort. The seasons follow each other year after year after year. No one is pressing a button, we don't have to put it into action, it just happens. The sun and the moon are always there; nothing holds them up; they just are.

- Your heart is beating; your lungs are allowing you to breathe, and your food gets digested. Nothing to do; it just happens effortlessly. Nature unfolds; we are part of nature, and everything just is.

- Are you what you are feeling at this moment? Or is there awareness of what you are feeling? Do you sense the difference between those two states of awareness? You are not your feelings. You are not your thoughts. You just are.

TOOL 2: CONSCIOUSNESS IS EVERYTHING. HOW IT CAN CREATE YOUR DREAM LIFE, ONE THOUGHT AT A TIME

Another tool to get closer to knowing your true nature is to become aware of your thoughts and find out where they're coming from. Are your thoughts coming from your limitless being or from your conditioned mind? Seeing the truth behind your thoughts will allow you to create your dream life by using imagination.

This exercise is much more practical. It can also help you with the first exercise if it is too esoteric.

There are two steps to becoming aware of our thoughts.

First, make an inventory of your thoughts.

You will need some free moments during the day, a notebook, and a pen.

The way to do this is by pausing a few times per day.

Sit quietly. Take a few breaths in and out.

Now, become aware of your thoughts.

Write them down.

I recommend that you set your alarm every two or three hours and just sit for five minutes and then write down what you become aware of.

Second, know that your results never lie.

Write down what is going on in your life.

Write down your health story, your money story, and your relationship story.

Because your thoughts create your reality, looking at your reality shows you what you're thinking.

Don't judge yourself.

Just become aware.

Look at your inventories, both for the thinking exercise and the result exercise.

Most of us will not like the results we see.

Now choose one story that you'd like to change first.

Would you like to change your health? Your financial situation? Or would you like to start with your relationships?

Create the story of how you want it to be.

Make it as vivid as you can.

Describe what you see, hear, feel, and smell.

Make sure you are the star of your movie, not a supporting character.

This is your life, your movie.

Read this story over and over again until you start thinking about it without effort.

I recorded my story and listened to it in the car, and before I went to sleep. I created a mind movie to make it even more vivid. You can find how to do that on my website.

Imagine your story as if it's already done.

When you do this daily, you'll see evidence of your story after a few days.

Keep going until your imagination becomes your reality.

The expression "Fake it till you make it" is not bad, but what you really want to do is: "Imagine it till you make it."

Good luck!

www.mindmastery.coach

Rika is a women's empowerment coach and Clearing Facilitator who will help you detach from your past and thrive. With 30 years of expertise in holistic tools, strategies, and mindset hacks, she'll help you take responsibility for your life and release the circle of blame and shame.

She started her spiritual journey more than 40 years ago while trying to figure out what her place is in this universe. She feels fortunate that at a very young age she already understood that there was more to life than what meets the eye. Rika is fascinated with both the seen and the unseen world.

She believes that everything is possible, that whatever you see around you is a reflection of what is inside of you, and she recently discovered the value of the gifts of our ancestors.

Rika realized her true nature and is determined to inspire others on their path of self-realization.

She is the founder of MindMastery; she teaches the laws of the universe and helps you to release old patterns and traumatic experiences so that you can start imagining the life of your dreams and live it.

Rika is a Proctor Gallagher Consultant, which allows her to bring the laws of the universe into small businesses.

Rika was born and raised in Belgium but moved to New York about ten years ago, where she lives with her two youngest daughters. She has five children and five grandchildren on both sides of the Atlantic. She loves traveling and cooking and started painting.

You can find what she is up to on her website www.rivkamarkel.com

"Our thoughts create our reality and that's all they do. Period."

~ Rika Markel

Chapter 10

FORGIVENESS MADE POSSIBLE

SACRED BOUNDARIES FOR SELF-CARE

Amber Kleid, Yoga Instructor, Mindfulness Mentor

MY STORY

I sat across the dining room table from my abuser. Only recently had I found the strength inside myself to come forth and ask the burning question, "Why?"

The damage was done almost 40 years prior, but it still festered in the dark shapes of anger and distrust inside my thoughts, actions, and whole being. It left a trail of broken relationships, self-hatred, and food addiction in its wake.

My inner clock told me it was 1 a.m. and fatigue was settling in like a warm blanket. The conversation we were about to have was purposefully waylaid by multiple stops at grocery stores and malls since I'd arrived six hours prior. I understood why. This wasn't a conversation I was excited to have either, but it was one I geared up for my whole life, and I'd be happy to put it behind me when it was over.

The moment the words, "I don't know," tumbled from their lips the world around me paused. It took me a moment to register what I heard. Blankly, I stared at them thinking, *Asshole, why can't you own it?* Disappointment shriveled my confidence and as hot tears escaped my eyes once again, I felt they had the upper hand.

After I arrived home, it took a long time to process the conversation and allow myself to grieve the idea that I may never have an answer. Yet, one year later, as I was enjoying a lazy day off, I received a phone call.

I heard, "I've been seeing a therapist."

With a quiet, cracked voice, I was told something horrific. I closed my eyes and my breath entered my lungs long and slow. The emotion tangled within their words resonated deep within me and the sting felt fresh. As they struggled to continue I offered a sincere, "Thank you for sharing with me. I understand how difficult this is and how hurt you must feel."

There it was, I received my answer.

Not long ago, I'm positive I'd have turned to the scathing thought: *They deserved every bit of it.* Instead, with a heart full of growing compassion, I offered three words that would propel my healing onto a path I never saw coming.

"I forgive you."

With relief I stepped out of the box I'd been a prisoner in as a frightened child, an angry teen, and a young adult woman who lacked responsibility for her own motives and truths. After waiting so long to feel justified, it dawned on me that no matter what the answer could have been, it didn't have a damn thing to do with me. I was free to let go and to start believing in the competency of my own choices.

My backstory begins when I lost myself.

At the tender age of seven without fully understanding the depth of what triggered my food addiction, batches of cookie dough were hidden in my closet enclosed in a Zip Lock bag to consume away from prying eyes. Boxed brownie mix was feverishly devoured like a last meal, and Tang was scooped right out of the jar so I could feel my buried emotions dissolve as the dark orange sugar crystals melted away on my tongue.

During Christmastime I honed my secret food consumption skills at my best friend's house. Her mom made the most amazing fudge I'd ever tasted and she purposefully hid the pan inside the hall closet. Amid heated Ms. Pacman competitions I excused myself to use the bathroom, and like a ninja, through a slight crack in the door I slipped soundlessly to lift the lid and inhale deeply before grabbing the biggest piece.

I can only describe the waft of luscious sugar mixed with butter and chocolate as the power that propelled me into a blind eating frenzy. The first taste was exquisite as I felt the sugary shock ripple through my entire body. The gobbling that ensued was filled with a numbness that grew into embarrassing waves of shame—shame that stared back at me in the mirror as I poked at my belly fat.

You're so disgusting. Why can't you control yourself?

I'd suck in my belly and calculate how many calories to hold back so the five, ten, twenty pounds of fat that jiggled inside the protruding mound of flesh below my ribcage would disappear for good.

800 calories? 1000 calories?

I cursed the absence of light between my thighs and pressed the thickest fattiest part against my femur to procure what I perceived to be a normal thigh gap.

Ugh, why am I shaped like a box? No wonder my friend says I have turkey thighs!

I became a pro at erasing all feminine aspects of myself by wearing extra-large clothing on my medium frame. I talked like a sailor and hid behind loud laughter and self-deprecation. As I aged, I denied myself intimacy and quite often jealousy pushed lovers away leaving my heart raw with emptiness.

At work, due to a lack of trust, I marched through exhaustion and resentment while refusing to share responsibilities. I continued that pace until Lupus, an autoimmune disease, surfaced as my body fought to keep up with long work hours and the numbness fueled by too much drink and unhealthy food. Until then, I was oblivious to the damage I was doing to myself.

In 2013 I had no idea who I was or where I was going when my journey to become more mindful of the ways I tended to my life started to unfold.

In my 20s, I came to the ancient modality of yoga for exercise, and not the healing medicine I use it for today. My practice was sporadic at best, but because of that diagnosis in my early 40s it became a constant in my life.

Eventually, it provided me with an unexpected transformation of mind, body, and spirit.

Each day I rolled out my mat to invite mindful breaths into my constricted body as it unfolded into shapes that felt like well-earned rewards rather than punishment for lack of self-control. I felt the strict boundaries around my self-hatred melt as my muscles stretched and engaged in ways that can only be described as deep sighs.

It's okay to let go.

It's okay to feel, soften, and accept yourself just as you are.

Thank you, Amber. Thank you.

My ego graciously stepped aside to allow this strange sensation of love for myself to fill my broken cup with guiding light. Each practice was a tiny step toward forgiving myself for overlooking this priceless gift—a magnitude of wonder inside a human shape.

It has been a decade of setting my own sacred boundaries by figuring out what makes *me* feel good and offering gratitude for every moment I've been gifted to try. I can barely identify with that overweight and undernourished person I let myself be *by choice.*

I've discovered a deep-rooted connection to my inner self and feel something far bigger than anything I can comprehend, working to see my journey through to the finish line, which, by the way, is constantly moving and grooving to keep me on my toes!

Had I not put forth the effort to show up for myself, I'd still be a prisoner to my victim mentality—blaming and shaming, holding myself in the anger of my past, and never choosing to grow personally or professionally.

Two years after my yoga practice began, I found myself in that seat at the table across from my abuser. A year after that, I washed my hands of that pain with the flow of compassion. The following year, I left a thankless career to teach yoga because the impact yoga had on my life was too profound not to share.

As I continued to play with and explore my boundaries, the rewards continued to pour in. Relationships that no longer served me fell away and I empowered myself to join Food Addicts Anonymous, a 12-step program for food addiction. As you read this I've been sugar free for 30 months and counting, and that alone is a miracle I believe saved my life. I took a month-long solo trip to India to feed my soul, and as I allow it, I know life is only going to present me with more opportunities to grow.

Yoga has become so much more than movement for me. My practice is full of connection and challenge. It demands discipline and self-study. It teaches compassion, humbles my spirit, and the exploration of mindfulness that unfurled has been most helpful. It allows me to be in the moment with clarity when seeking to lay down my own boundaries and encourages me to encompass my decisions with kindness and compassion.

What do you consider to be your most sacred boundaries?

I invite you to take inventory of your own wants and desires to build a foundation on which to lay the blueprint for them to materialize. Let this fun exploration be a guide as you learn to put yourself first. If you're a people pleaser or aren't used to making your own decisions, setting sacred boundaries for yourself while leaving out important people in your life can feel extremely uncomfortable. Know that experiencing that feeling is okay, and I hope you'll feel safe expressing yourself here. No one but you needs to see the finished product you cultivate, so enjoy the exercise below and let it be all about lighting up *your* beautiful soul.

It's likely that thoughts around the big picture and what-ifs *will* pop up. If you feel overwhelmed step away, center yourself with a few breaths, and return with a clear mind. This is exciting! There are a million reasons to say "Yes" to yourself and soon you'll see them unfold before your very eyes.

Grab your journal and favorite writing implement and put on some soft background music. Let your heart be open to infinite possibilities.

Please take a comfortable seat and close your eyes. Relax the soles of your feet on the floor, soften your shoulders away from your ears, lengthen your spine, and draw in a deep breath. As you release it with a sigh, let your belly button pull toward your spine to empty out your lungs completely. Feel your energy soften towards the earth as your next expansive inhale happens effortlessly. Repeat until you feel a sense of relaxation and groundedness.

Open your eyes, and let's begin.

THE PRACTICE

SACRED BOUNDARIES FOR SELF-CARE

1. Jot down one to three things that you dream about owning or experiencing. Imagine they've already happened. What kind of support felt nurturing on your journey there? Who did you turn to? How did their support feel to you? How does the experience feel to own?

2. Draw a big circle in the center of a fresh page. In the center of that circle write the word "WANT."

   This circle represents your boundaries. It's like the dance bubble Baby demanded from Johnny in *Dirty Dancing*. This is your space to explore what you desire and the feelings and actions that'll help you get there. Mapping these out first is an important step to pave the path to your desired destinations.

   Here are a few examples from my own bubble: I want the freedom to say "yes" when it feels right. I want to feel a profound love for myself and share my experiences to help others grow. I want to travel the world while deepening my spiritual connection with the Divine. I want relationships that feel nurturing and empowering and are in line with my greatest intentions.

   Put on some music and go to town writing down all your desires— no erasing! Your first instinct is usually the best.

3. When you're finished, write the words "DON'T WANT" outside of your boundary bubble.

   What doesn't serve your wants right now? Be honest about any emotions or feelings that might cloud the path to your desires.

   My examples: I don't want to feel frustrated or stuck. I don't want to have a trail of "shoulds" behind me. I don't want to have a victim mentality, feel disempowered, or be attached to outcomes.

4. When you feel complete, choose one of your wants, find a fresh sheet of paper, and write it at the top. Give yourself ample time to move through the next section of journaling prompts below because stinkin' thinkin' thoughts like, *it's too hard, this seems impossible, this*

is taking forever, and, *there's no way I can do this,* may pop up. Yes, it might be hard, it might seem impossible, and it does take time, but there's always a way.

It's said that when you meet with resistance, you're in the right place. So if that happens, take a few deep, slow breaths and venture forth, letting your list of "don't wants" guide your way on your first step to emotional freedom and setting sacred boundaries.

JOURNALING PROMPTS

1. At this moment, who am I while this want is *not* in my life?
   a. How do I act and feel?
   b. What *are* the impacts it carries on myself, my family, friends, co-workers, clients, and the community?
2. What magical being will I *become* when I am granted my *want*?
   a. Revisit a and b above with fresh eyes
3. What or who is blocking me from getting what I *want*?
4. What is one teeny tiny step I can implement today that will get me closer to taking ownership of this *want*?
5. Schedule it, set a timer, and get an accountability partner. Make it happen!
6. Rinse and repeat with as many *wants* as feels good.

Great job! If you have the energy, jot down a few notes about how your answers are making you feel right now. What emotions have come up? If mentally you can't quite nail down what you're feeling, turn to your body. It's the best barometer to help you connect to your emotions so check in with yourself. Do you have butterflies, is your heart beating a bit faster, are your cheeks flushed, or is there something else?

Come back to make adjustments, additions, and/or subtractions to your boundaries circle anytime you feel like it. You can make it colorful, add pictures, and even frame it to hang in a place where you'll see it every day as a gentle reminder to keep showing up for your highest desires in life.

I'm so grateful to you for reading my story and giving thought to building your own sacred boundaries. It takes courage to show up for yourself!

If you'd like to be prompted through this exercise, I've recorded a video for you to follow along with on my resource page, www.amberkleid.com/MMresources, that includes more goodies to help you become mindful in your mind, body, and spirit.

Amber Kleid is the owner of Kleidoscope Yoga LLC, in the beautiful mountains of Western North Carolina. Her yoga certifications include 500 RYT, 200 E-RYT, and she holds a level 2 Reiki certification. Amber is an expert workshop leader, mindfulness mentor, yoga instructor, and Reiki practitioner who combines the powerful wisdom of yoga and mindfulness to help people navigate their way to nourishing self-care. An empath, artist, author, cat mom, and explorer of new destinations near and far, she's a firm believer that we hold the power to heal within.

Amber's workshops, full moon circles, and mentoring sessions teach the building blocks of mindfulness, how to create sacred boundaries, how to hone your deep listening skills, utilize mindful eating and visualization techniques, cultivate an at-home yoga practice, and use meditation, dancing meditation, breathwork, conversation, curiosity, and compassion as powerful tools on the path to healing oneself.

Her yoga teacher training students learn from a light-hearted, consciousness-based approach about the importance of holding space, the potency and healing properties of restorative yoga, and how to lead classes for clients with chronic pain. Her teaching specialties are slow flow and restorative.

Off the mat and in her free time, you'll find her hugging trees along hiking trails, floating wistfully on her SUP board, loving on her cats Phife and Jolly, reading multiple books at a time, writing at her fave local coffee shop, cooking Indian food, dancing like no one's watching, and getting artsy to her heart's content.

Learn more about Amber, her journey, and her mentoring sessions here: www.amberkleid.com

Connect with Amber:

Facebook: www.facebook.com/akleid

Facebook: www.facebook.com/kleidoscopeyoga

Instagram: www.instagram.com/kleidoscope_yoga

Email her anytime: kleidoscopeyogallc@gmail.com

"When you rise to the spirit within you who knows what you're capable of! You are limitless."

~ Amber Kleid

Chapter 11

A CASE FOR QUIET

A MINDFUL HOMECOMING TO YOUR MOST AUTHENTIC, CONNECTED SELF

Jeanne Lauren Smith

MY STORY

"Yo soy alta y fea."

I sheepishly gestured to a picture of myself on a poster board I was exhibiting. I looked out at my classmates, their faces a bit aghast and surprised.

With just a basic understanding of Spanish, I managed to insult myself in front of the entire class.

"Hehe," I nervously laughed.

It was my high school Spanish class, and I was giving a presentation about myself. "I am tall and ugly," is what I chose to share, gesturing to my picture with the added intention of showing, *see, por ejemplo.*

Great, that was awkward, that didn't land, oh well, this is stupid, I'm stupid.

Self-effacing humor seemed like a good idea. If it was what others thought of me, I might as well beat them to it. Let them know *I know.* That they can't hurt me. "Sticks and stones may break my bones, but words will never hurt me." What? Words hurt. I internalized the words that hurt me as a form of protection. I didn't know I had armored myself at that moment. I thought I was being funny.

But it didn't feel funny. It felt weird. But in my weird, I felt a bit of a "who cares," too. Who cares about all your social norms, your pretending, and your fakeness? "Your" meaning everyone. The hypocrisy I saw on a daily basis in the world around me felt painful to experience.

"Move out of my seat you ugly piece of crap."

Sixth grade. New school. Middle school. Even though my elementary school funneled into this one, I might as well have been a brand-new student. The year before, fifth grade, was a great year for me, made great by the obtaining of the ever-elusive "best friend." Nerissa was smart, pretty, and kind. Every year she and her family of two brothers put on a magic show as part of the school assembly talent show. Full-on magic, and like any true magician, they never revealed their secrets. You might find this morbid, but I used to fantasize that if I were on my deathbed, then as my death wish, she'd finally share her magical secrets with me.

Having a best friend was everything I ever wanted. I felt safe, seen, and inspired. When her family moved to a distant suburb—30 minutes away—I was heartbroken. Starting middle school felt like starting over from scratch, without the felt sense of familiarity, security, comfort, and companionship of having Nerissa by my side.

"Get out of my seat, you ugly piece of crap."

It wasn't even my school district or bus route. My mom visited local elementary schools years before and petitioned to put my sisters and me in a neighboring one because she liked the set-up of the classrooms more and the education they offered. I decided to take the bus to fit in. I didn't want to miss out. I already lived a distance from everyone else I was going to school with. I yearned to have a community of friends to play with on my street, in and out of each other's houses with the freedom to roam and explore. I lived on a circular street at the top of a steep hill, so it was dangerous to venture outside the circle. There was only so much running around in a circle one could do, especially without any playmates nearby.

Once I thought I heard the melodic pull of an ice cream truck outside and proceeded to run around the circle over and over, only to discover, much to my disappointment, that it must have been a neighbor's wind chimes.

"Did you hear me? Get out of my seat."

My throat tightened and my face got hot. He stood over me, looking down with piercing eyes like daggers with a mission to destroy. I sat stiff as a board, hoping to become invisible. If only Nerissa had taught me how to disappear into a cloud of smoke.

"What are you doing sitting here? Who do you think you are? You don't even know anyone back here."

I peered over and pointed diagonally a couple of rows back.

"I know them. I'm friends with them. I know her and her."

Amy and Jill. The only familiar faces, freckled, with strawberry blonde, iron-straight hair. They sat with each other nonchalantly, unmoved by the scene. We played soccer together a couple of years previously, another failure in my attempt to be "normal." I was one of those kids who *hated* when teachers threw candy as a reward, for fear of not being able to catch it and suffering the consequences of the humiliation of another ultimate deficiency during adolescence, not being good at sports.

I remained stuck, immobile. I know I didn't move my seat despite the hostile command that I do. I didn't know the jerk with puckered lips and brown hair who bullied me, but his message was clear: *You don't belong.* And at that time, possibly even worse: *You're ugly.*

When I first tried to meditate, I thought it would be a breeze. I largely identified as "chill." I also figured, worst-case scenario, that I could fake it. *I have plenty to think about, so if it comes to that I'll just think about all of that,* with the idea that this would somehow be a productive use of time.

I'm in college taking a religion class. The assignment: Go to a service of a religion you haven't participated in. I have long been interested in Buddhism, so I find this the perfect opportunity to check it out.

As I kick off my shoes at the temple in Manhattan's midtown and enter the open space, I know I'm not in Kansas anymore. There is little if any instruction during anything that takes place, just doing, and gong-ing, and chanting.

As I sit on the cushion, it feels like an eternity. My back is screaming. It's excruciating. My mind is racing—*what is happening, how much longer can this be, I can't do this, this is horrible, what am I supposed to be doing, what the fuck is going on?*

The sound of the bell is a welcome relief from the constant chatter and the storm I feel inside.

It takes many more years, learnings, mistakes, and forgiveness before I'm able to take the time to rest and be still with myself.

As counterintuitive as it is, I used to think knowing about meditation, mindfulness, and being in the present moment was enough without actually doing it. I was inspired by the book, *Wherever You're Going, There You Are* by Jon Kabat-Zinn. The title alone felt like a *yes. That makes so much sense.* He recommended 45 minutes of sitting practice a day. Wait, what?

Again. *What am I doing? What am I supposed to be doing?* I hear thunder in my ears as the energy moves up into my nostrils and the space behind my eyes, flushing my face with a rush of heat and warm tears flowing down my cheeks as my body shakes. It's too much to close my eyes and sit.

I don't even know why I'm crying.

What's wrong with me?

I'm doing this wrong.

I hate myself.

How did it start? When was the moment I stopped knowing what was true, what had always been true? That I belong. And you belong. And our lives are miracles. And we're not broken, we're not fundamentally flawed, and we have nothing to prove—That our lives can be an opportunity, an expression, an offering, a gift. I didn't know what the meaning of life was.

The meaning of life. I remember in high school my close friend Kate shared a potent moment with my older sister, Michelle, asking her that question in the stillness under a sky of stars. She confidently responded, "To glorify God."

What was I missing?

"Things were never easy for you," my mom once told me with a compassionate tone on the phone when I was trying to put the pieces of the puzzle together. "You struggled with making friends."

I struggled with friends, and I struggled with myself. When I think of what made me want to be an actor, it makes perfect sense. I watched a black and white movie musical with the chorus dancing up and down the stairs, pointed at the screen, and said, "I want to do that." My beloved mom signed me up for dance class the next day.

Rhythm, singing, moving, connecting. We humans used to treasure these activities as a community. Surely many cultures and communities still do. Together we co-regulate our nervous systems and dispense stagnant energy. Choruses breathe together, and when we breathe together, our hearts beat together. When babies are held and rocked and see a stranger across the room bobbing up and down with them, they exhibit more pro-social behavior toward those that move in unison with their rhythm than those who are off-tempo. In a study, when the people they connected with over movement dropped an object, the 14-month-olds took the leap to save the day and retrieve it for them (Cirelli, Wan, and Trainor, 2014).

Rhythm, singing, moving, connecting. I manifested for myself a lifelong practice that would bring me into connection with the people around me.

But what about myself? My interest in meditation came full circle when I felt the urge and desire to live a more meaningful life—to live in integrity and to stop the cycle of giving and receiving pain to and from those around me. After breaking my own heart and those of others. It wasn't until I had tried every other coping mechanism—relationships, sex, drinking, and a tunnel-vision pursuit of success—to try to bring myself back into balance, that I was finally able to give the cushion a chance in a real way.

"Things were never easy for you" might have been an observation of me as a nearsighted three-year-old with trouble pronouncing my Rs, entertaining myself with the company of My Little Pony and imaginary stories instead of human friends; yet it repeated itself in those first several years of being out on my own and waking up to myself as an adult when I still felt like a child.

This time, to my delight, there was at least some instruction. "Bring your awareness to the breath. When you notice the mind wandering, gently note 'thinking,' and come back to the breath."

Simple, but not easy.

As I continued my mission to live with more intention and integrity, I became more and more open to approaching my life as a participant, and not a victim. Simple lessons like "I create my own reality" opened my eyes and uplifted me. Knowing I didn't have to believe my thoughts was a balm to my anxious soul. My practice helped me learn how to spend quality time with myself, become my own best friend, and enjoy my own company—to not have to fill every silence and to not, at long last, measure my value based on what everyone else thought of me.

I began to like myself more, and this new environment of self-compassion and understanding created the possibility for deeper relationships, artistic expression, healing, and forgiveness for myself and others to emerge. I used to look at myself in the mirror with so much judgment and disappointment, but now I was meeting my own gaze with love and compassion. I recognized my inner and outer beauty and no longer diminished myself as a form of protection.

Seeking out and creating drama in my life no longer appealed to me. I stayed focused and intentional even among the extreme challenge of waiting tables in fast-paced New York City restaurants.

"How do you stay so calm?!"

"I meditate before I come here."

Of course, I still got angry, frustrated, and defensive, but these reactions no longer carried the same weight. Cultivating a daily practice helped improve my clarity and my perception of reality. It's like going to the eye doctor, "This one," the sound of a shutter *click,* "or this one," *click.* "Option A," *click click,* "or option B." That difference of clarity in being able to see something—a thought, a situation, a reaction—is the difference between running around in circles, chasing an ice cream truck that isn't even there, to realizing the source of the sound and deciding to stop. To recognizing choice. I have a choice in how I respond, and how I engage.

Breath by breath, wandering thought by wandering thought, I began to put the pieces of myself back together, even the ones—especially the ones—I had long ago discarded with no intention of return. The picture became clearer. And as I slowly integrated my mind, heart, and body, a growing peace and inner reservoir of tranquility, strength, and stability became my home. In giving myself the time and space for quiet, I found self-acceptance on the other side.

I used to think a successful life would be one without regret. Now I know I can make mistakes and face the reality of the situation. I can apologize, make amends, forgive, and vow to move on forward and better. That "perfect" is an illusion and one I don't have to live up to. I can allow myself to be a human living a human life.

THE PRACTICE

The practice is simple. It's an offering to ourselves. How do you let people around you know that you love them and care about them? You give them the gift of your presence, a listening ear, and your undivided attention. That's what we're doing here. We're treating ourselves like we matter because we do. Like we're our own best friends. I don't have to travel back to fifth grade to feel seen and deserving and cared for. Meditation teacher Kate Johnson says, "Meditation is making friends with yourself." And it is.

Little by little, any hardening that has happened in defense of the lie that you're not worthy of your own attention begins to soften. The resistance to accepting yourself just as you are begins to melt away. Of course, self-judgment and insecurities will still arise from time to time, but we can see those habits as what they are, misguided attempts to keep us safe and secure. They still come from love. We deserve to give ourselves the time and attention we give to our best friends. We can start with this simple offer.

Open to what's here

Feet on the ground

Feel with openness and curiosity

Ease and self-compassion

Reflect

Meditation can be done in a stationary position, seated, standing, lying down, or walking. For this practice, I invite you to choose a stationary position. It could be on a chair, a cushion, lying on a mat, or on a bed.

Whatever works best for you. To support you in your practice, you can access an audio recording at https://www.subscribepage.com/offerdailypractice.

Beginning this practice by *opening to what's here*—tuning into the sounds around you—taking in the space around you. What does this moment taste like? Taking some time to settle into the present moment. Open to what's here.

Bringing awareness now to your *feet on the ground.* If you're seated on a chair, I suggest that you feel your feet flat on the ground beneath you. But wherever you are, notice the feet, the heels, the contact points, and allow this to bring your awareness to the space below you, the connection to the earth, and allow yourself to feel held and supported by the earth.

As you're ready, begin to *feel with openness and curiosity.* Noticing whatever you can feel all along the surfaces of the skin from head to toe: the contact points of your seat, feet, and hands. The air temperature on the skin, the movement of the breath in and out through the nostrils or parted lips. Inviting in your openness and curiosity as you take some moments to feel.

Beginning to invite a sense of *ease and self-compassion* into your experience, whatever it is. Knowing that whatever you're experiencing is welcome. As a gesture of ease and self-compassion, you may like to place a hand or both over the heart or gently stroke an arm. Allowing these qualities to envelop your experience with a sense of spaciousness and understanding. Embodying a sense of ease and self-compassion.

Staying here as long as you like.

Beginning to close this practice, opening to the space and sounds around you, sensing the feet and the connection to the earth, taking a moment to *reflect* on this period of practice, and offering yourself gratitude and acknowledgment for taking this time to be with yourself in a kind and supportive way. Reflecting on the causes and conditions that led you here, that made it possible for you to practice in this way today. Reflecting on how you'd like to show up for yourself and others for the remainder of the day and inviting in any intention that comes up around that. Reflecting on any other insights that arose for you that you may like to explore further.

As you're ready, gently open your eyes, lift your gaze, and begin to take in the shapes, colors, and space around you.

What did you notice in your practice? Mindfulness is about paying attention, but also *how* we pay attention, so invite in these qualities of ease, compassion, openness, and curiosity as you reflect on your experience. There is no wrong way to experience this. I want you to know there is room for whatever it is that comes up for you.

Thank you so much for sharing your practice with me today. Feel free to contact me anytime. I'd love to hear about your practice and discover how I can best support you in your journey. It's my priority to help us all in creating a sustainable practice that strengthens our growing connection, grounding, and emotional availability towards ourselves and others. I don't want anyone to be stuck in cycles of shame, doubt, and self-judgment. Holding the vision for us all to come to know the truth that we are whole, we are worthy, and we matter.

References

Cirelli LK, Wan SJ, Trainor LJ. Fourteen-month-old infants use interpersonal synchrony as a cue to direct helpfulness. Philos Trans R Soc Lond B Biol Sci. 2014 Dec 19;369(1658):20130400. doi: 10.1098/rstb.2013.0400. PMID: 25385778; PMCID: PMC4240967.

Jeanne Lauren Smith is the founder and facilitator of As You Are Mindfulness and the creator of the online course Reclaiming Quiet, empowering women to reclaim their inherent dignity through exploring the power of quiet in themselves and all aspects of their experience. She helps anyone looking to feel more connected, grounded, and emotionally available towards themselves and others in developing a sustainable mindfulness practice so that they can release the negative impacts of stress and gain resilience, inner peace, and confidence in their daily lives.

She holds a BA in Theatre with a concentration in performance from Marymount Manhattan College. As a lifelong actor, she has extensive experience working with various modalities in movement, breath, voice, and developing presence. She completed Yoga Teacher Training at Arhanta Yoga Ashram in India in 2013. She has been practicing meditation consistently since taking an introductory class in 2014 and knows the joy of developing a daily practice. She has facilitated group and 1:1 virtual mindfulness sessions and retreats since September 2020 and completed her teaching certification through Engaged Mindfulness Institute, which emphasizes sharing mindfulness in a trauma-informed way.

She resides in New Hyde Park, New York with her husband, Dominic, and sometimes with her two stepsons, Nicolas and Jake. Originally from the Pacific Northwest, she is an enthusiast of coffee and the color green. She is happily alcohol-free and enjoys a good mocktail. She loves nature, dancing, and traveling.

Connect with Jeanne:

Linktree: https://linktr.ee/jeannelaurensmith

https://linktr.ee/asyouaremindfulness

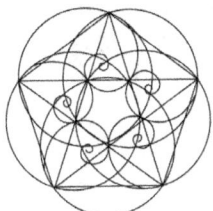

"When we come into deeper and kinder relationship with ourselves, we in turn are more easily able to emotionally resonate with others. This is part of the reason that taking this time for our practice is not only a gift to ourselves, but to all those around us as well."

Jeanne Lauren Smith

Chapter 12

ALIGN TO YOUR PURPOSE

HOW TO MANIFEST WITH WRITING

Tiffany McBride, MA, LCPC, ORDM

MY STORY

*"Be impeccable with your word. Speak with integrity.
Say only what you mean."*

~ Don Miguel Ruiz

In 2015, I was on my third burnout in the agency field as a licensed mental health therapist, living paycheck to paycheck, and could barely afford my bills as a single woman. I had just moved into my own house and wanted to learn to be independent without having a partner. But instead, I felt stuck, hopeless, and depressed.

I graduated with my master's degree five years before and studied and worked tirelessly for my clinical license. I had already burned out as a foster care counselor, then as a therapist at a residential teen facility, where I was on call 24/7. Now, I was burning out as an outpatient therapist for a community with very little to no resources. I didn't feel like I could help people by allowing them to talk about their trauma repeatedly with no helpful tools—especially when their current life wasn't getting any better.

Every morning, I struggled to get out of bed and felt like molasses getting through each session. I was required to see eight clients a day per quota, or we were lectured about it. I prayed for clients not to show or cancel so I could have a mental break from all the horror stories I kept hearing. I felt cooped up in this little office, sitting all day, just listening.

Sometimes I would accidentally zone out, completely missing what my clients said.

"Tiffany, are you okay?" asked one of my clients.

"Yes, I'm fine," I lied.

"It looked like you were zoning out there," my client responded.

"I'm sorry. Please continue talking," I regretfully said.

The tools and modalities I learned in my training did not work for the types of clients I saw. Many of these clients were on welfare, chronically and critically mentally ill, and heavily medicated. These were complex trauma victims, and the tools I utilized weren't helping them.

Secretly, I began working part-time on the side to start a psycho-spiritual practice. I wasn't allowed to have my own practice because it went against my agency's policy. It was a betrayal of their no-compete contract. But I desperately wanted to do things differently in the mental health field, be a little more eccentric, and expand into the world. I saw what didn't work in western mental health and wanted to bring in more of the energy practices that helped me face my traumas and mental anguish.

Meditation, essential oils, being in nature, starting yoga, learning about crystals, astrology, metaphysics, practicing tarot, and utilizing herbs and plant medicine have become exceptional skills to help regulate my nervous system. Also, adding movement/exercise, diet, bodywork, energy psychology, and writing helped me feel better. These things included the mind, body, and spirit of a person. However, I couldn't practice these modalities in the agency as they were not evidence-based or clinical approaches.

I sought out my mentor, who was teaching me about energy bodywork.

"Words have power!" Sue, my mentor, mentioned. "Have you ever heard of Dr. Emoto?"

"No, I don't believe so," I replied.

"Dr. Emoto claimed that human consciousness could affect the molecular structure of water. He experimented with water molecules to show how human thoughts and intentions can physically alter the structure of water. The water crystals could be altered simply through conscious intention. The results were crazy. For example, positive words created these beautiful water crystals, whereas negative words resulted in the opposite effect; the crystals were discolored and deformed. They have done the same experiments with plants and jars of rice." Sue showed me the differences between the positive water crystals versus the negative water crystals.

(See https://thewellnessenterprise.com/emoto/ for more information on this project)

"Wow, that's amazing!" I stated.

"So, since our bodies are made up of 60 to 70 percent water, how do you think our words and thoughts affect us?" She asked.

"Uh! Probably a lot," I replied.

"So my question is, do you speak kindly to yourself and others? Or do you struggle with this?" Sue asked.

I pondered for a second. I struggled with extreme self-doubt, anxiety, and obsessive-compulsive thoughts then. I allowed toxic relationships to dictate my life. I believed anyone who said "follow me," which only led me into financial and emotional trouble. I struggled to have boundaries and did not know how to care for my own needs or desires.

I felt anxious about what others thought about me, and I believed I had to have a man behind me to have a successful business. I had a few male partners who tried to run my business into the ground. I allowed them to rule my choices because I didn't know how to assert myself.

I was unkind to myself every day in the mirror and compared myself to others constantly. I hid behind people pleasing and always being happy or the perfect one. I couldn't get my mind to stop racing with all the horrible things that could go wrong, such as being abandoned, or judged, or if something would break down or I wouldn't have enough money to pay my bills. I began to struggle with all sorts of addictions so I could tame those monsters.

I told Sue, "The water in my body is probably deformed shit. I'm not nice to nor do I believe in myself." I paused. "Oh no, what does that mean?"

"It might just mean you have to change how you talk and think. Words not only manifest within our own bodies but into our reality."

"Do you think that may be why I struggle with these pains and chronic issues?"

"Possibly. Would you describe pain and illness as discolored and ugly looking?"

"It feels like poison to my body," I stated.

"And possibly your life. How often do you repeat the same story in your head that plays into your life?"

I thought about her question. I tend to focus on the abuse from my parents and how I'm not lovable. The lack of support and extreme neglect left me craving attention and love. However, I continuously picked relationships that repeated the stories of abuse and neglect, over and over again. I felt alone all the time, and there was a deep hole in my heart that so badly wanted to be filled.

I replied, "So, like, how I struggle with my past abuse and subconsciously pick the same type of relationships that mirror or re-trigger that wound?"

"Yes, that's a great example. And what if you could change that story?" Sue asked.

I looked at Sue sideways, "I don't even know how to do that," I said.

"How do you feel about writing?"

Writing has always been a form I used to express myself since I was a toddler. I remember watching my mom write when I was young, and I'd scribble on pieces of paper and pretend to write cursive like her. I wasn't allowed to have writing utensils, but I would sneak them into my room anyway. I grew up writing poetry, songs, and short stories. This led to writing scholarly papers and articles for academia and my career.

"What would I write about?" I questioned back.

"Well, whatever is happening in your mind at the moment. It can be all over the place, as that is how our minds work. Most people tend to spiral and flip. The point of this exercise is that after a few weeks, you can read back on your writings and identify the themes that hold you back from the life you want. This is the first step to mindfulness and understanding our thought patterns. Once you identify the themes, the negative cognitions, the old stories, and the dreams, you can break them down into categories. But you won't know until you see the repetition."

After that session, I began writing in a journal and identifying the habits, blocks, people, and themes keeping me from focusing on my goals and dreams. I obsessed over having a romantic partner and got lost in fantasy instead of focusing on what I wanted.

However, I didn't know what I wanted until I looked beneath the obsessions. I saw that I had wants, needs, and dreams. I wanted to be an independent contractor, I wanted to be a blogger, a published author, a teacher for workshops, and share psycho-spiritual modalities with people. I wanted to see people heal themselves by using their natural resources within. Outside my career, I wanted to travel and explore other countries and societies. I wanted to feel confident and respected by others, especially men.

I approached my priestess teacher Ruth one day. "How do you cut or eliminate the things you don't want in your life?"

"Word magic," She stated.

"Word magic?" I questioned.

"If you could identify one thing, person, or belief that keeps you stuck from what you really want, what or who would that be?"

"My ex," I said quickly.

"So I want you to write everything your ex makes you believe about yourself, the triggers around him, and the traumatic memories associated with him."

I began to write down a list of things and filled the page with words and phrases.

I'm too loud. I'm not heard. I'm not important. I deserve pain. I must be the perfect partner. I must cater to his needs to get attention. When he ignored me. When he would hurt me physically. Silenced. End of my music career.

"So, are these the things that keep you stuck, hurt, and would you like to cut out?" Ruth asked.

"Yes, I would say so."

"Okay, since you are cutting this out, now there is room and space to replace what you are cutting out." I looked at Ruth, confused.

"So, for example," Ruth read over my list of words I wanted to cut out, "he negatively impacted your dream of being a professional singer. How would you change the story? Would you replace that with incorporating singing back into your life?" Ruth asked.

I instantly rolled my eyes.

"What was the story you just told yourself as you rolled your eyes at the idea of singing again?" Ruth asked.

I stopped and thought. *Yeah, right, I'm too old; it's too late now.*

"Write that down as something you want to cut out, and on another piece of paper, write positive things like?" Ruth looked to me for the answer.

"It's never too late to start. I am a singer. I love singing. I can learn to sing again." I professed.

"Perfect."

"Okay, and then what?" I asked.

"I usually take a string and tie the "cutting list" to one end and the "want list" to the other side. Cut the middle of the cord, eliminate the old negative shit, and invite the new. Then throw them into a fire to release the magic."

"That sounds like some woo-woo stuff."

"Well, I did call it word magic," Ruth smirked at me, and I laughed.

Even though I identified blocks, worked through my traumas in therapy, and utilized my psycho-spiritual techniques, I still had no direction, and my mind and body became depleted.

By 2017, I reached my finale in agency mental health. I could no longer mentally or emotionally continue. I felt helpless since I couldn't aid anyone to grow or heal, and morally I felt I was doing a disservice to myself and others when I knew a better way to heal. I quit without savings or a plan and began working part-time, recovering from burnout, and building my practice by starting a business plan called The Road Map.

Using my signature plan, The Road Map, I became aware of my blocks and identified my dreams. I learned to cut attachments to people and distractions that kept me from my true desires. I struggled when I lost my job and house and filed for bankruptcy. However, that needed to happen to get out of a bad business deal and contract I previously made.

I began asking myself tough questions about who I was and what I valued. I created a vision and mission to help me focus, and made a plan for my goals. I surrounded myself with teachers, mentors, and good energetic people who taught me the skills I needed to become a healer, businesswoman, and author. I read thousands of books and went to all the workshops.

I worked really hard. I lost friends. I was homeless at times. I had to deal with not-so-great experiences and healing sessions. I met healthier people. I asserted my boundaries when I was afraid of abandonment or rejection. I failed. At times, I worked every day with no days off for weeks at a time. I made mistakes. I loved, and I lost. I dove into my shadow work daily, so I could master myself and make friends with my demons.

Now that it's 2022, at the age of 39, I have my own successful integrative private practice; I teach workshops, write published books, travel the world, and live my life the way I want without a partner by my side.

I feel self-confident in who I am; I love who I have become. I'm in love with the freedom in my life and being financially stable. I can assert myself appropriately, and I am respected by many people in my community and around the country.

Writing has been a great way of manifesting my life path, a magical tool, and an old friend that has gotten me through anything.

I ask you to be patient with yourself and let this take its time. It took me seven years to get to a successful place, and I'm still growing. Word magic takes time to manifest and to align your mind to your purpose.

Below I offer the first step to building your own road map.

THE PRACTICE

THE ROAD MAP TO ALIGNING AND MANIFESTING YOUR LIFE

You must work through these steps slowly. Word manifestation and planning take some time, along with brain power. Begin writing your daily pages for three months before starting the cord-cutting practice.

1. Awareness and Self Discovery

Begin to write three pages a day.

(Allow three months of daily pages before going to the next step)

- Journaling is a fantastic mindful tool. Mindfulness is slowing down the mind and becoming aware of our thoughts, emotions, patterns, and stuck traumas. It helps us to pause and take a breath.

- Become aware of the themes, negative cognitions, old stories, hurts, pains, dreams, desires, and wants in your pages.

Cord-cutting, inviting word magic.

(Inspired by my teacher Ruth Souther)

- When you recognize the themes, cognitions, and traumas, you can start to write down all of those mentioned on a piece of paper. Once written down, take a separate piece of paper and write down what you would like to replace those negative energies with, such as new hopes, dreams, and patterns you'd like to bring into your life.

- Tie each piece of written paper on each end of a string. For example, negative cognitions are on one side, and dreams and positive patterns are written on the other side of the line.

- Light a candle or fire.

- Send intentional thoughts, prayers, spells, or heart energy to your cord and cut it in the middle. Throw each piece of string with paper into the fire to be released.

- You will see and feel the subtle effects of this technique over time. Please allow time between other cord cuttings (one time a month is encouraged).

Take the time to answer these important life questions.

Begin to ponder on these questions after three months of writing three pages a day. Allow this to unfold however you feel is right for you. There is no time frame for this exercise.

1. What would I want to experience in life if time and money were not an issue?

2. How do I want to grow?

3. What do I want to contribute to this world?

4. Who am I? Why am I here?

5. Where am I going? How do I want to be remembered when I am gone?

6. If I achieved all of my life goals, how would I feel? How can I feel that along the way?

7. What is most important in my life? What do I value the most? What am I most passionate about?

8. What brings me the most joy and sense of peace in my life?

9. What does a victorious life look like for me?

10. What do others most admire in me? If you don't know, ask people who know you well.

11. What unique gifts do I want to share with the world?

12. What are my top five values?

13. What are my top ten achievements in life?

This only brings us to the first step in my signature plan, The Road Map. There are nine more steps to go moving forward and if you are interested in learning more about how to unlock the secrets to the rest, please reach out to me at https://www.tiffany-mcbride.org/contact and request a free PDF/ link to The Road Map! I am also available for coaching if you would like to join my Road Map Program.

Tiffany McBride (She, Her, They, Them) is an LCPC, Reiki Master Teacher, birth doula, expressive artist, and author. They run their private practice named Holistic Vibrations, LLC. They use holistic remedies and altered states of consciousness for those who struggle with trauma, addictions, women's issues, LGBTQAI+ support, and those seeking a deeper spiritual connection. Tiffany is currently working on their Doctorate in Shamanic Psycho-Spiritual Studies and is training to be a yoga teacher and a clinical hypnotherapist.

Their holistic and altered states of consciousness modalities include Emotional Release Therapies (utilizing energy/positive psychology such as EMDR, EFT, MBSR, etc.), expressive arts therapies, energy healing with a foundation in Reiki, womb healing/doula services, sexual health education and empowerment, attachment trauma recovery, internal family systems, inner child healing, codependency recovery, motivational interviewing, transitional life coaching, spirituality, breathwork, hypnosis, somatic psychotherapy, and psycho-education.

Tiffany hopes to eventually grow a community healing arts studio to help more people learn to express themselves and heal from their traumas and addictions. In Tiffany's downtime, they love to write, blog, paint, draw, play the ukulele and guitar, sing, be in nature, kayak, take photographs, read, go to concerts, hang with friends, and be a forever student.

Connect with Tiffany:

Website: https://www.tiffany-mcbride.org/

Instagram: https://www.instagram.com/witchycrowwmn83

Psychology Today:
https://www.psychologytoday.com/us/therapists/
tiffany-mcbride-bloomington-il/454372

Music Page: https://www.tiffany-mcbride.org/artsrhythm

"Words have Power!"

~ Tiffany McBride

Chapter 13

PARENTHOOD VS. CAREER

HOW TO FIND A MINDFUL BALANCE

Anuka Garaza, MA, PGDip

MY STORY

"You are pregnant" he said with a wide grin.

I began to notice some hints of yellow in between his incisor teeth. All I could feel was numb. I just remember feeling both alone and afraid. I was at my gynecologist's office in Geneva, Switzerland. I made an appointment with him because I was experiencing some pelvic pain, and I attributed it to previous urine infections, which I was accustomed to when I grew up in tropical countries during my early childhood.

I wasn't expecting this moment. I thanked him and quickly and made my way out of his office, desperately trying to find a quiet space to find a moment of reflection and pause.

In many ways, nothing about this experience should've been a shock. I was a young professional and married, and this was something my husband and I had discussed and said we wanted. But like many professional young women at the start of their early career, I decided to be on the contraceptive pill for so many years that I didn't believe I'd get pregnant so quickly. I was constantly told and reminded by many medical professionals during my annual check-ups that if I wanted to get pregnant, "it would take some time." Incredibly, this moment of surprise and fear wasn't going to leave me for some time.

It was this experience that brought me closer to my deeper inner self in a way I could've never imagined. After the shock and surprise and sharing the news with my husband, I started to embrace the journey of pregnancy. I was a naïve young mother. I wasn't sure what to expect. Although my mother was a midwife, I come from a family dynamic where my mother never really shared any knowledge or wisdom about her experiences of pregnancy. I was pregnant, young, and living in a different country from where I grew up, and although that never mattered to me before I was pregnant, I suddenly felt quite alone and vulnerable. I often found myself embracing a fetal position on our bed, just pondering in a dark room, not conscious of any particular thought but feeling this sense of being lost, with a cool numbness flowing down my body.

This was the moment I consciously turned to my mindfulness practice and experience in meditation for presence and stability. I was often asking myself the question, *what type of parent would I be?* Would I be enough? I noticed many thoughts drifting from one negative bubble to the next. Look at you, I thought, wasting time feeling sorry for yourself when you should be savoring this moment with gratitude and love. What an opportunity to be a parent! Of course, these constant thoughts berating my every move also made me reminisce about my own childhood upbringing. Growing up in North London, my parents struggled to support us. They often worked multiple jobs when I was a child.

However, we did spend family time together, and I remember most fondly when we visited a local Buddhist monastery in the beautiful English countryside in a town called Hemel Hampstead in England. There were many weekends when we'd offer our time to cook in the community kitchen or clean the public spaces in the monastery, such as the shrine room. These were the moments at a very young age when I knew there was something important about observing the peace in sitting still. I remember watching the monks for hours and thinking, *how do they stay seated and still for so long?* My five-year-old little body wanted to rebel and move constantly. And yet those few moments where I did allow myself to feel the stillness, I felt like I was connecting more to myself. Looking back, this was probably my unconscious start toward my spiritual growth as a parent.

I remember the early years raising our daughter tested every part of my being. Mentally, was I stimulating her enough with the right educational development? Physically, was I challenging her enough with baby massage? Or, during her toddler years, was she interacting enough with other children? Emotionally, was I a balanced mother? Was I present enough for my husband; was I cultivating a healthy balance between motherhood and work? Without really thinking about myself in a conscious way, when I think about it in hindsight, I was probably experiencing constant emotional parental burnout during the first five years of my parenthood.

McKinsey reports that "the stress of working from home added to the seeming unrelenting responsibilities of caring for children and families has been overwhelming for many working parents, some of whom describe feeling as if they are losing it or going crazy under the pressure."

I think it's important for us as parents to understand and accept that no matter what your education, profession, or ethnicity, if you're in a caring role, parental burnout is a syndrome resulting from chronic stress that *anyone* can experience.

SIGNS AND SYMPTOMS OF PARENTAL BURNOUT

We all know the difference between feeling agitated by something or feeling full-out anger when we're triggered. In my experience, as parents, if we're not self-aware, we can tend to ignore the disruptions our heightened emotions play on our children or dependents. The result of this behavior impacts our children's growth, sometimes contributing to emotional deficiencies in adulthood. We as adults can imprint emotional pain into our children in their early years, and the effect of this is that we may create hardened hearts, or a condition the late psychiatrist David Viscott called "emotional debt." In my experience, however, learning and processing my past emotional wounds from my own childhood has helped me manage myself when I experience parental burnout. My recommendation to you, dear reader, is to read this list and take time to study and observe how some of these symptoms of parental burnout feel in your body:

- Feeling isolated and consciously withdrawing from others
- Feeling anxiety, overwhelm, or excessive mental suffering
- Feeling resentful (either to your children or someone of meaning in your life)

- Not wanting to be touched or feeling alone
- Feeling guilty all the time
- Wanting time to yourself all the time
- Experiencing constant bad sleep
- Experiencing changes in your appetite

If you're experiencing any of these signs or symptoms, you may be experiencing parental burnout. These signs and symptoms may indicate that you should seek professional help. I strongly advise this, even if you're thinking, *but I don't think I feel these signs often, but I have in the past from time to time.* There is a practice I wholeheartedly believe you can cultivate with mindfulness and compassion, which may help you start your healing process and cultivate resilience simultaneously. It starts with mindfulness.

THE PRACTICE

WHAT IS MINDFULNESS?

My favorite definition of mindfulness comes from Jon Kabat Zinn, the founder of Mindfulness-Based Stress Reduction, who says: "Mindfulness is awareness that arises through paying attention, on purpose, in the present moment, non-judgmentally, in the service of self-understanding and wisdom."

With this practice, I really do feel *intention* is the key. Ask yourself first, what is my intention with this problem/challenge/situation? Especially if you experience what I felt in the earlier part of my journey of managing parental burnout, where I felt moments of inadequacy or ill-equipped to manage these feelings.

It is, however, also important to understand that what I'm about to share with you is not a miracle practice. These suggestions will not change your state of mental and physical burnout immediately. But if you allow it, it may equip your mindset with clarity and agility you may have never experienced before.

I often found remaining centered and letting go of any personal psycho-analysis is helpful when having the intention of creating simpler self-awareness through mindfulness. When I intentionally decided to embody peacefulness as part of my parental being, I allowed myself to be open to a wave of compassion and love for myself. This gives me great resilience when I face challenging behavior from my children. Of course, things get complicated, and emotions sometimes get ahold of us! When we feel anxious, this sometimes also causes us to blame either ourselves or others for causing this distress. But believe me, my friends, when I experienced those blame moments, I always felt that the emotions manipulated and controlled me. However, when I used mindfulness to ground me, it allowed me the spaciousness to accept the blame. It also offered me an understanding to process where these behaviors and thoughts originated from. I noticed many of my conditional thoughts about being a parent were based on reflections from earlier childhood memories. Parenthood is not a game of who is right and wrong. I felt the mindfulness-based coping strategies below helped me when experiencing 'emotional debt.'

MINDFULNESS-BASED COPING STRATEGIES

1. Speak your mind

   It's normal to feel like past experiences or comments made to you by loved ones or acquaintances make you feel like you cannot share your innermost concerns or anxieties. However, I felt reaching out to a trusted person with intention always complemented my mindfulness practice by feeling grounded.

2. Find self-compassion within

   Find self-compassion by understanding your parenthood. Being a parent is hard. I try to tell myself often: This is a hard moment; you're experiencing a moment of difficulty. Allow yourself some grace and kindness.

3. Take self-care breaks

   Try and find creative ways, moments in your day, to appreciate something good and positive. Maybe a fantastic cup of coffee or appreciating the sense of warmth when the sunlight hits your face. Share a romantic meal with your partner. No matter what the act, make sure it has nothing to do with parental duty and something to do with you finding joy in the moment.

4. Finding purpose

One of the reasons I decided to write about my parenting story is because finding meaning within myself about myself gave me a sense of something greater than myself! It gave me perspective when I felt like my life was spiraling out of control. Mindfulness meditation on a daily basis, whether five minutes or one hour a day, has the possibility of grounding you in the moment and giving you a prosperous moment of peace and reconciliation with whatever you're facing.

We need to remember, as parents, we always have a choice. Yes, we all have childhoods and experiences that contain good and bad moments. Sometimes, they are unfortunately reflected upon us by our parents and sometimes by our communities, schools, or friends. Whenever you allow mindfulness in your life, you allow yourself to find your inner self-rights. You discover how sometimes moments from your past have carried over into adulthood, taking different forms. They can create self-blame or anxiety, and you may sometimes find yourself blowing things out of proportion. When you practice self-awareness through mindfulness, you're maintaining constant vigilance. This allows you to speak from your values and truth rather than reacting.

Over the years, we've learned as parents to cope with or prevent workplace burnout. However, the COVID-19 pandemic has created mental stress and strain on our lives and our children's lives like nothing we could've imagined. Time has become even more precious. So has trust—trust and wisdom in our body and the willingness to use mindfulness to help us cultivate trust and openness.

WHY COMPASSION IS A POWER TOOL FOR PARENTHOOD

When you notice you're not in alignment with your mind, body, or even the essence of who you are, my advice is to stop. Meditate on your breath moving through your body. Feel the sensation of your breath expanding throughout your body. Take time to prepare for your meditation. Try and find a place that is quiet and reasonably dark if possible. Allow yourself to center yourself using the sensation of the breath. Use something you associate with joy and peace in your life if you cannot use your breath and decide to use visualization instead.

Compassion for yourself flows through all the energy centers in your body. If you allow it, compassion meditation suffuses your heart. It radiates brightly throughout your body. For most people reading this, it may seem strange to think how valuable compassion can be to being a parent. The knowledge I've found through compassion is its ability to help you meet a higher consciousness within yourself and, therefore, a higher motivation that helps you reach your ideals of personal power. For some, this may seem too spiritual to digest. I understand. I don't expect you to buy into this notion of compassionate wisdom immediately.

My suggestion would be that after you finish reading this chapter, remember that compassionate wisdom can help you in your parenting journey by helping you overcome those moments of powerlessness or burnout. Compassion can be a powerful agent of change in your life. You'll see for yourself how compassionate intention combined with a mindfulness practice helps you discover an instinctual intention and strength in how you envision yourself as a parent.

You may compare this thought to how athletes relate to flow as "being in the zone." A compassionate parent is a parent who works from their own harmony, purpose, and being. You may feel a sense of lightness in the body; you feel carefree and joyful. If you experience any of these sensations, you're allowing compassion to help you connect with a kind of bliss consciousness within you. We are so used to setbacks, obstacles, and failures in our modern lives that we sometimes get blocked by only negative perspectives. However, when we utilize mindfulness and adapt compassion, we create a shift in awareness and connect to a deeper intelligence as parents.

I remember clearly, the first time my daughter's school called me when she bit another child in kindergarten. I remember my entire day being filled with shame, blame, and parental guilt. My whole day of stress was based on external factors. In this state, I found my energy scattered on so many fronts—analyzing my work schedule and debating if I had done enough to talk to her about appropriate behavior at school. Maybe she wasn't happy and acting out—had I missed something?

But when I focus on my mindfulness practice, I only focus on the self, my inner self. There is nothing to keep up. I maintain a clear and open mindset. Compassion helped me pick myself up when I faced setbacks. It brought me into a deeper mindset, took me out of my mental struggle, and helped me find clarity rather than exhaustion when confronting what would be helpful to finding success in parenting. I no longer felt mentally burdened or anxious.

The themes of this chapter—parenting, mindfulness, and cultivating compassionate wisdom—have unfolded throughout my story. It's natural, as we face a post-COVID-19 world, to feel overwhelmed with fear for the uncertain times ahead of us as we try to support and raise our children. We tend to find solace in spirituality or higher wisdom only when we're facing despair, especially in the west. My conclusion and solution are to connect with your inner wisdom using mindfulness when trying to find your true self as a parent. The joy of the present moment is where you'll find the deeper strength, wisdom, and clarity you seek as you take step after step in your parenting journey. My journey has made me a conscious parent. I've learned it's important to trust your heart in every aspect of parenthood. One of the greatest gifts we bring to our children is our dedication and intention to bring forward their goodness and cultivate their potential. But my greatest advice is never to forget yourself in this process. Be true to who you are, use mindfulness to embrace that journey, and burnout will never again be a negative struggle in your parental journey.

Anuka is dedicated to helping individuals navigate their mind-body connection when faced with adversity and mental pain. A global citizen who was born in the UK and has lived in Sri Lanka, South Africa, Switzerland, and the US, she brings cultural awareness, human sensitivity, and spiritual compassion to all of her coaching and leadership offerings.

She has spent the last two decades studying, practicing, and coaching mindfulness. As a coach, Anuka is dedicated to supporting individuals with practices that unlock a new way to be when faced with personal and professional challenges. She believes that cultivating emotional intelligence skills is an accessible way for everyone (and especially parents!) to make the necessary shift to grow, heal, and empower themselves throughout their journey in life.

Anuka spends most of her time coaching professionals and individuals, utilizing her own life and leadership experience. Most recently, she has been working with women in leadership roles—helping them to hone their curiosity and embrace their purpose as they face growing pressures in their everyday routines. She also teaches leadership programs with Inseus LLC for Fortune 500 organizations across the US and the world.

Connect with Anuka:

Website: https://www.janujoyfulservices.com

Website: https://janujoyfulservices.com/home/mindset-mastery/

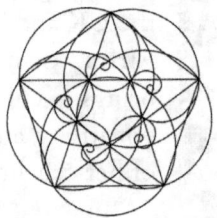

*"Every time you allow mindfulness in your life
you allow yourself to find your inner self-rights. You discover
how sometimes moments from your past have carried over into
adulthood taking different forms."*

~ Anuka Garaza

Chapter 14

MANIFEST

USING NEW MOON ENERGY FOR YOU AND YOUR HOME

Dr. Christy Robinson

MY STORY

DR. T'S OFFICE

I sat in Dr. T's office, as I had many times before. "If I gave something up in my life, would I get better? Do you think I'm doing too much in life to heal my body, Dr. T?"

I wasn't expecting the answer that soon followed. I was expecting confirmation in the way of, "Yes, of course, Christy. That would help tremendously. Do that."

Instead, she looked at me with swords of clarity in her eyes and delivered truth in the kindest, most compassionate way.

"Christy, ever since I've known you, you have had several wheels spinning at the same time. It is almost like ADD, always doing many things at once. But it's not ADD." Then, her eyes met mine and the swords dug in deeper. "Christy, what are you running from?"

WHAT THE HELL JUST HAPPENED?

I had competing thoughts running through my mind, met with the vulnerability resonating deep within my soul like a powerful storm.

What am I running from? Shit, am I running from myself? But I've done my work, my mind argued with itself. *I wasn't trying to prove anybody wrong. No one called me lazy when I was a kid. Was I trying to justify my own worth with achievements and a revolving door of unending new projects? I am going to help everyone else. I'm a psychologist. The whole purpose of my work is to help others through their pain, loss, and fear.*

THE TRUTH

Shit, I've been running from myself, my pain, and the innocence that was lost to death. I knew I could never look at life the same after being orphaned, so I just wasn't going to look at life at all. I was on autopilot. Maybe I was running from what life could look like if I just loved myself and my pain enough to finally heal it.

WHY DO WE DO THIS?

Distraction can be our friend. It can also be our enemy. And most of the time it's a silent one. We're often not even aware that it's happening. Our defense mechanisms are so deeply embedded in us that we dress them up in nice clothes and call them overachievement, perfectionism, dedication to my family. It really is avoidance of yourself, your self-compassion. It is easier to distract ourselves with things than look at ourselves in a way that might disrupt our life. Disruption is always uncomfortable, but it can also lead to things far greater than you could have imagined for yourself.

As women, we're taught that others are more worthy of love and attention than we are. How often do you just sit with yourself and be? There's no judgment coming from me here. Hell, I did an entire doctoral program this way to deal with being completely alone after losing my family. We all like to avoid pain because it requires that we see some things about ourselves we might not like. When we can tolerate the quiet and feel what is in our hearts, then we can experience peace.

Eventually, you must face yourself. You must love yourself. Only then can you truly love and heal others. Our feelings must be acknowledged, not avoided through distraction. I want you to be free. I want you to release all of the limits you place on yourself.

THE MOON CYCLES CAN HELP YOU HEAL

When I was a teacher, one of the elder teachers said, "It must be a full moon today." *What is she talking about? She's been teaching for too long.* I giggled to myself and went on with my day. Out of sheer curiosity, I started tracking the full moon each month and charting my student's behavior in the classroom. Damnit, she was right. It makes sense. The moon is strong enough to move the oceans and control the tides. It can certainly handle us humans. Learning to work with her cycles helps us harvest her power and manifest better.

The moon goes through five phases each month during its orbit of the Earth. Just like its effect on the oceans and tides, the moon affects our emotions too. It can bring things to the surface and give us a chance to both call in and release things in our lives. The new moon phase is a chance to start over fresh each month and manifest new things into our life. What are you ready to manifest in your life? This is the time to set your intentions.

THE THREE KEYS
TO WORKING WITH THE MOON ENERGY

GO INWARD-THE FIRST KEY

Intuition is a form of knowledge that comes from the subconscious mind into the conscious mind. Often, much of the information we take in is registered in our brains without our conscious awareness. Have you ever turned down a street because it's part of your normal daily drive, even if you weren't going to work that day? This is the brain's subconscious at work. Eventually, you realize that you turned on the wrong street.

Intuition and intentional reflection are great bedfellows. A quiet mind is a receptive mind. Meditation is a great way to harvest intuition. Many people fear tackling meditation because they feel it requires sitting in silence for hours with a clear mind. This is not the case. I love guided meditations because they do the work for you. Walking in nature is a great way to ground and meditate. Essentially, the purpose of meditation is to quiet the conscious mind so the unconscious can speak to you.

EGO OR HEART

The part of intuition that is so critical is to trust what it's telling us and act on it. The logical, conscious brain is the enemy of intuition. It houses our fear, which comes from the ego. It will override what we know to be the right decision. The ego often thinks it's protecting you when it can hold you in patterns that no longer serve your life.

You must differentiate between the conscious brain and your deeper intuition. Your body and mind are closely connected on a subconscious level. How do you feel in your body when you think about a certain decision? Does your body tense up or does it relax and feel peace? If you feel peace in your body, your intuition has spoken to you. Have the courage to act.

BOUNDARIES AND SELF COMPASSION-THE SECOND KEY

PROTECT YOUR ENERGY

Everything is energy. Energy expresses itself in many forms. Some are positive and some are negative. Because of this, we must be very careful about what type of energy we always allow around us. To do that, you must learn to distinguish between good and bad energy. Most importantly, your life will be influenced by the type of energy and people you spend your time with most frequently—you attract more of what you're currently putting out to the Universe. The Universe does not care; it's all the same to it. If you want more negative energy, keep sending negative thoughts out to the world. If you want more abundance, express the energy of abundance and you will attract even more of it. Surround yourself with good energy and watch your life amplify in the most magical way.

The irony in having good energy is that everyone wants some. They need your energy. Recognizing this when it happens and being able to put boundaries in place will change your life. You don't have to cut anyone completely out of your life, although you can if you feel that's what is needed. But you can learn how to control the amount of time and energy you give these energy vampires. You can still love someone and limit their role in your life.

HOW ENERGY WORKS

Qi (chi) is contagious. Have you ever met someone and just walked away thinking, *ick,* but you had no idea why? This is dirty energy. We read energy on a subconscious level, and those who are early in their energy journey will feel this but not be sure what it is they're sensing. Ever hang up the phone feeling exhausted and drained because all the other person did was talk about themselves?

These people are energy vampires. They will take all your energy and leave you feeling depleted without you knowing what hit you if you don't have proper energetic boundaries. A quick and easy fix when you need to suddenly shift your energy back is to run very cold water over your hands and arms up to your elbow for a minute and literally shake off the negative energy.

As a psychologist, I studied under a renowned trial forensic psychologist here in the States and here's what I learned—much of what is communicated between people is not spoken. In fact, we default to the unspoken to know the truth about what a witness, juror, or defendant might be saying. Our brains have learned how to twist the truth to either please others or to protect ourselves. However, the subconscious part of the mind, which controls all your non-verbal behavior just can't lie. One of my favorite things is when you ask someone a yes-no question and they respond yes while shaking their head to the right and left, indicating no. Which is the real answer? You guessed it, it's no.

My point with this: we come into this world with this ability, and we slowly diminish it as we go through life and learn with the conscious brain. It wants to protect us and often adapts in ways that hurt us in doing so. Children and dogs have the purest most truthful energy because they have not lost it yet. Have you ever met a child that didn't tell you exactly the truth, no matter how it might hurt your feelings? Or a dog that couldn't sense someone not safe to be near their owner? They are masters at reading energy. So, think with your energy, not with your brain.

Learn to be aware of how your body reacts to stimuli wherever you go. Once you master this, you learn your energy needs. If your shoulders are tense, your body is talking to you about a situation, person, or place. Listen. The longer you ignore it, the louder it will get. Unfortunately, this is how disease sneaks up into the body. If you ignore it long enough, the body will get your attention.

ENERGY VAMPIRES

Page was calling on her way home from work. I was so excited to talk to my friend after the day I had. I wanted to share my news with her! I eagerly picked up the phone and said, "Hey girl!". Uh-huh, yeah. I know. Thirty minutes had passed, and I was drained. I had not got to say one word about my news. It was finally my turn. Yay! "Christy, I've got to jump off; my son is calling."

Energy vampires are like heat-seeking missiles for empaths. To be fair, not all energy vampires realize what they're doing consciously. They're just trying to get their unmet needs met. Empaths often fall into this because of their desire to heal others. We think we can love the world and make them better.

Identifying the energy vampire starts with reading the energy of others and listening to what you feel in your body when around them. Mind and body connections should always be developed, and the stronger this is, the better you'll become at recognizing vampires. They take energy from others to sustain their own needs and unplug when their needs have been met, regardless of your needs. These are the people that call you and talk about themselves for 30 minutes then say goodbye leaving you to wonder why you even answered the call.

You must be so careful in selecting what you give your attention to daily. You also need a home that supports you a hundred times more than the average person. Self-care is essential for you to thrive in life. Grounding your energy daily, spending time in nature, clearing negative energy from your body and home, and cutting cords to toxic people are all things you can do to set energetic boundaries. Taking time to recharge your energy is your responsibility and it's not selfish to do so.

Simply put, a boundary is giving yourself permission to say no to someone else without guilt or shame. It means realizing your needs are just as important as those of others in your life. It's saying "yes" when we want to, and "no" when we do not want to, without sacrificing ourselves for someone else. It's realizing you are only responsible for your own emotions dear one, no one else's.

IS SELF COMPASSION THE MISSING INGREDIENT IN YOUR MANIFESTING?

Why do we find it so much easier to show compassion to others than to ourselves? So many of us are gracious, loving people to others in our lives but not to ourselves. This is nothing short of tragic because showing ourselves love and compassion allows us to show up in the world. For some reason, we feel guilt when we take care of ourselves. This is especially true for us women. I think we have a natural compassion that we freely give to others. Yet we were never taught that we could give that same compassion to ourselves.

When you learn to do this, something magical happens. You shift your energy into alignment. Guess what happens when you're in alignment with the Universe's energy? You manifest abundance in an amplified way into your life. This is truly your greatest tool in manifesting the life you want.

INTENTION SETTING-THE THIRD KEY

Those of us who study the brain and neuroscience have a fancy term for your ability to literally rewire your brain by choice. It's called neuroplasticity—the brain's ability to heal itself after injury and to rewire itself in response to repetitive thought changes. Yes, your brain can be wired to respond to a situation in either a positive or negative way based on your historical responses. So, take back your power. When a negative thought comes, say to yourself, *No, cancel that.* Then, reframe it in a more positive gracious way. Doing this repeatedly over time will change your brain.

THE OTHER SIDE OF INTENTION IS GRATITUDE

Gratitude is truly the key to manifestation. Whatever you wish to create in your life, it all begins with gratitude for what you do have. It sounds counterintuitive, but the less you have, the more you can be grateful. When I had lost just about everything in my life, I learned true gratitude practice. I learned to break things down to a very simple level and be thankful. I had my dog, a place to sleep, and food to eat. At that time in my life, it was all I needed. The more I resonated with an energetic state of gratitude the more abundance came to me in life.

In the law of attraction, this happens because whatever energy you resonate with, you'll attract more of. So, practicing simple gratitude will bring more of what you want into your life. Wherever you are in life, start there. Practice gratitude truly from your heart, believe in your power to manifest, and the rest will be done by the Universe. There's something so sacred and so pure about simple gratitude and mindfulness in life.

Something I love to create is a gratitude list for the people in my life. I list ten things I love about them and then share it with them. Not only does this help you express gratitude, but it allows those you care about to feel loved and appreciated. Hold onto this because it's a part of the practice to come later in the chapter.

INTENTIONAL CRYSTALS DURING THE NEW MOON

Crystals are pure magic in your home. They're the most powerful application of the earth element, and each has its own energetic imprint. Once you start working with crystals, you'll find which ones resonate with you the most and this will change over time depending on your needs. One of my most favorite ways to spend a Saturday is a trip to the crystal shop in town to see what calls to me. It's absolutely amazing to me that I choose the one with the exact healing properties I need at that moment in my life every time.

Crystals are very personal to each of us, and I always suggest picking them intuitively. Just look at the crystal and feel its energy. You can set your intention for what you want to manifest in your life and program it into that crystal. Then, let your crystal soak up all of the moon energy by placing it outside the night of the new moon. This will allow you to work with it long after the new moon has passed.

You can decide which moons you want to work with based on which astrological sign it is in that month. Each sign holds certain properties you may or may not want to work with. At the time of writing this chapter, we are in a new moon in Libra which is all about balance and harmony in our lives.

THE PRACTICE

Start with the basics. Self-care and self-love are not complicated. Quite the contrary, they're simply taking care of your needs on a basic level with plenty of love. Be patient with yourself.

Allow yourself to make mistakes. Allow the parts of you that are hurt to be seen, felt, and healed.

This is self-compassion.

Your home can help you with self-love in some great ways. Here is a list of things to do to show yourself some much-needed compassion. I mean you are amazing, right?

1. Buy fresh flowers and place them at your desk, entry, or in your kitchen.

   Choose flowers that you love and feel energized by.

2. Design your bedroom to support rest and restoration.

   Did you know this is the one room in your home most connected to self-love?

3. Take a salt bath. Pour some moon-charged water or essential oils into your bath that hold your intentions.

4. Prepare yourself a nourishing meal that feels nostalgic to you.

5. Work with plants and crystals that have the energy of self-compassion to energize your home in this way.

6. Find a cozy nook to read a book and sip a cup of tea.

7. Give yourself a nourishing facial care mask and skincare routine.

8. Turn the lights out and burn some candles just for you.

9. Do a guided meditation.

10. Express yourself through art, painting, music, and/or journaling.

11. Detox with an infrared mat, sauna, or smoothie.

12. Go offline and unplug all from all devices.

13. Purge clutter from your home.

LOVE YOURSELF

Do you remember that gratitude list we discussed? It was easy to think of ten things you're grateful for about the other people in your life. Now, I'm going to challenge you further. Make a gratitude list for yourself. List ten things that you love about yourself. These are not things you do for other people or things that others value about you. This comes from within you and only you. Take your time with this. It's okay if it doesn't come to you immediately. Put this list away after you make it and when you're having one of those days where you're judging yourself, get it out and remind yourself that you are fucking amazing.

Christy is a trained medical psychologist and Feng Shui Master who empowers women to live flourishing lives. By connecting their mind with their home through Feng Shui, powerful intentional change is created. She believes that you deserve to love yourself, your home, and your life.

Christy has been studying the mind for 25 years. In 2013, she began searching for healing modalities outside of western medicine. This is when she became aware of energy and started to study a wide range of other perspectives and philosophies. This journey led her to study under a leading Feng Shui Master. Here, she made the connection between the mind and home. During the pandemic, she realized the absolute necessity of creating a home sanctuary as a place of respite from the world.

With her training as a medical psychologist, she was able to connect the universal fears that we all experience in life and how our homes reflect what is going on in our minds. While studying Feng Shui, she discovered three ancient principles that could empower your mind, home, and life.

"Just like its effect on the oceans and tides, the moon affects our emotions too. It can bring things to the surface and give us the chance to both call in and release things in our lives."

~ Dr. Christy Robinson

Chapter 15

IT'S TIME TO DISCIPLINE YOUR INTELLECT

MASTER YOUR THOUGHTS THROUGH YOUR POWERFUL CONSCIOUSNESS

Eddie BenAbraham

Lifetimes of gratitude to my wise and loving parents Malka and David, my amazing brothers Isaac and Joe, and awe-inspiring Suns Ariel and Eytanel. Love you, always.

MY STORY

It was a night of nightmares, a high fever, and endless sweating. Both Mom and Dad were next to me, sitting on the edge of my bed holding me as I opened my eyes. It was the early morning hours in my tiny bedroom.

Springtime in Israel, the weather was getting warmer but without the heavy humidity of summer yet. I love that season; as kids, we ventured to odd locations and sought out different fruit trees that were ready to feed us their sweet and sour gifts.

As soon as I looked into my parents' eyes, I knew this was not just a bad dream. They looked worried but didn't say anything to show their fear. My older brother Isaac, was not there that night. He was the one who always protected me. This time it was Mom and Dad in full-on parental protection mode.

There is no way to describe the voices and sounds in my head. To this day, I remember the loudness. It was like my head was linked to a thousand people's heads. I heard them speak and shout all at the same time.

The chaos in my mind didn't stop quickly. The voices kept on going for days, possibly weeks, I don't remember exactly. One afternoon I said to my mom, "I can still hear the loud voices in my head." Very calmly, she replied, "Then tell them to stop."

As a result of that night, I was afraid to be alone in a room or enter unlit spaces. The darkness terrified me. I couldn't tune out the voices; however, what my wise matriarch said was accurate. I was about seven years old, and to this day, I remember the instances I consciously faced my fearful thoughts. I verbally pushed the voices away with stern, intent-filled order, "Go away, enough!"

This was not my first observation of thoughts and the power of our consciousness. My dad led me from a young age with his extensive knowledge, tremendous heart, and profound awareness. He was truly a man beyond his time.

However, this experience was different because there was an outside influence causing that night of influx. The energies responsible for that experience were not welcome. But, thanks to that night and what followed after, they helped build the foundation of who I am today.

Every day I faced them again and again. Then, one day, the voices simply vanished as if they were never there. I overcame my fears and worries by utilizing the power of *free choice*—truly a divine gift that we must learn to treasure again.

Free choice is the catalyst of life.

I've repeated this mantra in almost every session, class, and presentation. Our capacity to choose at will is the foundation of our experiences here on Earth.

Your responsibility is: *to choose.*

Because if you don't, the grand potential you came into this lifetime with will not be fulfilled. There's no wrongdoing from your soul's perspective. You'll simply return to work through these potentials in another lifetime.

I remember one very clear moment when I stood at the open entrance of the small bomb shelter in our apartment building. There is at least one in every structure in Israel. There were no working lights to switch on, only sunlight penetrating the cold and dark concrete staircase. For a long time, my neighborhood friends wanted to explore this particular shelter. It was the only one we didn't have access to yet. Even though it felt like my legs couldn't move, I wanted to join my friends and step down into this frightening abyss. It was one of the types of fun for us children who had the outdoors as our playground. That type of freedom may seem trivial to most children today; however, back in the mid-seventies, it was adventurous.

I was in the middle of a power struggle between my intellect and fear. *These voices must stay out of my head; I must end this cycle of thoughts and fears.* This was a critical point in my understanding of my capacity to be in the present moment without any inner distractions. Instead of allowing my thoughts and feelings to overwhelm me, I chose to end the battle. My consciousness is the overseer of my intellect, *The King.* My choice was simple: *Halt all of my thoughts and emotions related to past experiences and possible future outcomes.* At that moment, I walked down the stairs. I held that state of being for a few seconds until I reached the end of the staircase.

Two of my friends were already there, inside the shelter, speaking loudly: "We can't see much of what's in here; it's too dark." I quickly walked to the center of the cold and moldy-smelling room. I looked around as my eyes adjusted to the low level of light and glanced at what I could see. From what I recall, there wasn't much to see. The space was vacant and empty for a long time. There was nothing more I could explore, but I stood there for a moment, right in the middle of the dark shelter. I looked back to the staircase, seeing the bright light of the clear blue sunny afternoon. "I'm standing here looking outside. This room seemed so scary because I didn't know what was in it."

Later in life, this particular understanding showed up like this: *I don't know what I don't know.*

How often do you find yourself negatively entertaining yourself with the thought process called "What if?"

- What if I don't get paid?
- What if I don't find love?
- What if I don't have enough money?

- What if I don't get there on time?
- What if he says no?
- What if she gets upset?
- What if I gain weight?
- What if I get sick?
- What if I fail the test?

You can spend hours, if not days, adding to this list of perpetual fear and doubt. These types of thoughts are a common theme in the minds of many.

You must let these go and stop the endless loop of worry and fear.

Let it go.

You can use your awareness to identify specific thought processes that enter the present moment during your everyday experiences. It's a good starting point to get to work and begin the task of clearing these unwanted thoughts—judgment, fear, or any other thought processes no longer serving you.

One of the powerful methods of healing is done with your pure intent and gratitude: *Dear God, dear Creator, thank you for clearing the thoughts that no longer serve me.*

In contrast to the negative "What if?" you can practice positive ones instead. For example, here are subjects driven by love and positivity:

- What if I'm offered a better job?
- What if my client loves my service?
- What if my body heals quicker?

Or the one I love the most:

What if the outcome is better than what I can possibly imagine?

Think about the possibilities you open yourself to. You're instructing God to manifest what you desire in better ways you think are possible. Remember: *You don't know what you don't know.* The mighty all-knowing Creator knows infinitely more than what your finite mind is capable of conceiving. Submitting to Source, the ultimate leader, elevates you from the attachment of *time* and *how* things should unfold. This is not an easy task to accomplish, but it's one hundred percent achievable.

I must digress a bit because there are two fundamental components related to our main subject. They are self-love and synchronicity. The journey of self-love is the most important ingredient that you *must* include in your recipe for creating your reality. During the nine-week course "Ascending Into Your Heart's Awareness," I teach the fundamentals and tools that help expand your heart. The wider your heart is open to the love of self, the more profound your life will become.

Synchronicity shows up regularly in your life. Your job is to identify and act upon it. If you don't pay attention to the hints the Universe presents on a golden tray, you might miss an opportunity you were asking for.

This leads us back to—awareness.

Awareness plays a key role in our life. From the time our senses mature, we get on the awareness wagon. Identifying things in our reality through sound, touch, smell, and sight. When a baby takes its first breath, you are able to observe and identify the slow growth process of awareness. Identifying Mom's voice, feeling her warmth, the taste of her nourishing milk, crying when uncomfortable, or catching a glimpse of their subtle smile while they're dreaming.

As we grow, our awareness continues to expand year after year. Then, at some point, this expansion of awareness regresses to minimal development.

This doesn't mean that in our twenties, forties, or sixties, we cannot maintain a healthy expansion of awareness. Simply have the courage to choose for yourself.

With increased awareness, you can identify the synchronicities showing up on your path and take advantage of them. We're back again to the power of choice; you choose when a particular potential presents itself.

When I stood at the entrance of the bomb shelter, I was given an opportunity. The choice I made was the one thing allowing me the capacity to learn and heal.

It's time to share with you the premise of this chapter:

Expansive awareness is a powerful state of being. When combined with free will and self-love, your consciousness will create what you desire.

What is expansive awareness? It's your ability to maintain a growing capacity to receive more knowledge, comprehension, and, ultimately, wisdom. Expansive awareness can be practiced using all of your five senses and with your powerful *intuition*—your sixth-sense: The infinite source of knowledge and wisdom.

That night in my bedroom, the dream was frightening, and the days that followed were challenging. However, during this life lesson experience, I received a gift. Learning more about who I am in ways no one could've taught me. The intricacies of your thought processes are best understood when you consciously choose to learn.

There is no limit to what you can achieve because if you can think it, you will create it. The process of thought comes from the divine Source; it's present in every cell of your body and speaks to you through your DNA. You are the extension of Source; there is no separation between your physical reality, higher self, Soul, and the almighty Creator. No one other than yourself can tell your self what to think, feel, or choose. Yes, I'm aware of how we're bombarded by external influences, more so in the last century than ever before. However, ultimately you are the soul, the only one who has the right to decide.

You have the God-given right and duty to choose as you will.

Childhood experiences are the groundwork for the soul's growth and advancement. The contracts are made and potentials marked. That's when the individual's life path begins with the capacity to facilitate advancement and growth. Free choice is the tool we use consciously and subconsciously to take ownership of our destiny.

When you have options in life, it's called choice. But when you're given a situation, it's known as—*The hand of God.*

So the question is, do we really have free choice on all levels of life? The answer is yes. But it will be a challenging task in this short chapter to explain why.

However, I will say this:

Depending on your point of view, Earth's game-board of life can be understood as either good or bad. However, if you have a bird's-eye view, like that of the Creator, you'll observe humanity as a child learning to walk on its own. We're taking our first step towards independence and freedom.

The work we're doing individually—to heal our pain, fear, anger, and sorrow—is also healing the collective.

How did we make it this far? *We chose.*

We chose to stay and continue this marvelous game of life on Earth. It's the reason many are awakening. The Golden Age is almost here. We simply need to do some more lightwork to transmute the dark. The nature of the "dark" resides in the negative and feeds off the energy of fear, anger, and suffering, and because of this, it's not going to leave without a fight.

Discipline your intellect with the power you have inside you. Your consciousness will be grateful because life is so much calmer when you no longer actively reproduce negative thoughts.

If you are the extension of Source then you are one with your Akashic records, higher self, ancestors, and the rest of your *Entourage.* This means you have the freedom to learn anything you desire.

There is one challenge we're continually faced with—*time.* We think that things should manifest on the day, month, or year we want. God does not look at your clock. You must realize that your "meal" will be ready when it's cooked and ready to serve you. My father always explained: "Eddie, you must have patience. Because patience is very important for a healthy flow in life." My dad's mantra helped me on my journey, especially when I was faced with intense challenges.

Childhood is a beautiful thing because we evolve through life's biggest learning curves. With the help of our consciousness and free choice, our childhood years help us plant the "seeds" from our Soul-contracts. These so-called "seeds" or agreements manifest into reality as the various challenges in our life. Remember, you signed up for this work, and only you have the power to successfully complete it.

THE PRACTICE

We live on a planet that is aware, wise, powerful, and loving beyond measure. Mother Earth, Gaia, Imma Adamma, Pachamama and more. These are a few of the names our ancestors called her. Why do we perceive that our planet is female? The most common answer I hear is because of the incredibly abundant life she nurtured for eons. This does not mean that Gaia holds only feminine energy; there is a balance between male and female. It resides within every aspect of Earth's being-ness.

Gaia is a powerful sentient being who's been here, working diligently, to prepare for the arrival of the Divine Souls—You.

Today we'll teach you the process of release. The path to the lightness of your being. Gaia is your partner with the type of union that is multifaceted and goes back millions of years. The relationship you have with Mother Earth is a multi-dimensional melding that your mind can't fully grasp.

Even though there is a limit to what your thought process can see, when you expand your heart's capacity, you can achieve greater symbiosis.

Your connection to Gaia is profound and unbroken. It's what the indigenous tribes of the land knew for thousands of years. Today, your capacity to heal is far greater than ever before.

The following is a sacred ceremony given to you directly from Gaia. She asks that you find a private place where land meets water, preferably in the morning hours as the sun is rising. Sit comfortably in this space, close your eyes, and begin slow deep breaths.

Allow the time you need to settle into the rhythm of the place you are in. If you're at the beach, pay attention to the waves as they cycle onto the sand. If you're next to a river, listen to the water's swirling currents moving forward and around the boulders in their path.

When ready, speak the following to Gaia:

"My beloved mother, I am here to seek your assistance with my worries, fears, doubts, and sadness. I am ready to consecrate these moments with you. I am grateful for your love and healing."

Gaia:

> Sweet one, as you sit with me here in the sacredness of our union, I bring before you a silver tray. On this large tray, I ask that you place your worries, fears, sadness, or any other thoughts or feelings you wish to heal. Take your time to dive deep into the old fissures within your memories. Pluck away the old and unpleasant. Take them all: The events, decisions, and imprints, and then gently place them on the large silver tray.

I ask that you do not hold back and do not disconnect yourself from the emotional waves you're experiencing. These are important to process as you lay every memory on the tray. Allow the tears to flow, let the anger expose the pain, and welcome the feelings to run through you—*one last time.* I am here to hold you strong and with unfathomable love.

Your choice to relieve yourself from the past is key to your advancement and mine as well.

As you sit in these moments of love and healing, complete your release, and then I ask that you remain as you are. Clear your mind, clear your thoughts, and neutralize your feelings. For as long as you desire, be present in these moments of stillness so I can do the work on you.

I now take away the silver tray and all that you have placed on it. Releasing you from your past is a process that is powerful and profound because you are melding your consciousness with mine.

As it should be my sweet child. Your healing is complete.

I bid you fulfilling days ahead.

~ Gaia

Dear Soul, this concludes my chapter. I invite you to learn more about these subjects through my main website: Vort8x.com (Pronounced Vortex). There you will find classes, courses, sessions, presentations, and more.

I'm grateful and honored you are here.

Infinite blessings

Eddie BenAbraham

Eddie BenAbraham is a teacher, channel, healing facilitator, inventor, presenter, and author. In 2019, Eddie built Vort8x. com with a mission to assist fellow humans during the shift into Earth's new Golden Age.

Through his teachings of basic and advanced esoterics, Eddie offers his tribe the awareness and the means to consciously create a life of joy, balanced health, and abundance.

"My Entourage" is what Eddie calls his divine-support team. Using the art of reading Turkish coffee grounds, Eddie's channeled sessions and coaching programs give an in-depth reading and can lead to profound realization and healing in your past, present, and future. One of the key subjects in Eddie's powerful courses and presentations is "The Anatomy Of Your Soul." This subject has been a passion from a young age, and today, it has developed into a critical part of understanding the divinity in our human experience.

In 2017, Eddie introduced to the world one of his inventions: "The Compassion Gauge Tool." with the help of his friend and master programmer, Peter Bakalov. The Compassion Gauge Tool can automatically detect and measure the level of compassion. Once the user clicks the button, the system recognizes their state of being and, in a fraction of a second, shows the level of compassion ranging from 1 through 10.

Eddie's most recent development is his connection with The Seven Founders - The Original Whales. The fascinating channeled information will be part of a six-book series—five workbooks based on his course, "Ascending Into Your Heart's Awareness," and the sixth about the Original Whales.

Eddie's ongoing work includes a wide range of subjects. You're invited to join the loving community on his online platform to connect with like-hearts. There you will find the services offered and ways to contact Eddie directly.

Please visit www.vort8x.com

We look forward to meeting you.

"If you didn't have what it takes to accomplish what you came here to do, you wouldn't be here."

~ Eddie BenAbraham

Chapter 16

CONNECTING WITH YOUR INNER CRITIC

A BULLY-FREE FUTURE STARTS WITHIN

Amy M. Wisner, Ph.D.

MY STORY

THE BYSTANDER

I will never forget the day I sat idly at a classroom table next to three eight-year-old girls who were unmercifully bullying my friend Garrett. The girls quietly chanted, "Garrett is a girlie girl, Garrett is so gay. Garrett is a girlie girl, just make him go away," while simultaneously kicking his shins under the table. All three girls mocked him. All three girls kicked him. And I sat in silence.

Garrett looked at me with pleading eyes as if to say, "Amy, why aren't you helping me? I thought we were friends."

We absolutely were friends.

And yet, I did nothing.

Garret was a sweet, small, and quiet third grader who wore thick glasses and a bow tie. His bike was equipped with a cassette recorder duct-taped to the handles that played a recording of the computerized voice of KITT, the infamous 1982 Pontiac TransAm Firebird driven by Michael Knight (David Hasselhoff) on the show "Knight Rider."

When Garrett and I rode around the neighborhood on our bikes we often stopped so he could press the hard, plastic play button to hear the staticky sound of a fictional TV show robot car recorded next to the speaker of his family's antenna-style television. He was proud of his invention, and I was fully supportive of his KITT-inspired bike.

I didn't have the foresight at eight years old to know why "Knight Rider" was Garrett's favorite show. I now realize it's likely because the main character sought justice for the innocent, helpless, and powerless victims of bullies who were seemingly above the law. Garrett needed to be his own hero because no one else was defending him. Not even his true friend, who actually loved hanging out with him.

Forty years have passed since that incident, and I still get sick to my stomach when recounting the story. In fact, if I tell the story aloud, I always cry.

Why was I such a coward? Why didn't I protect my dear friend from those asshole kids who were tormenting him *right in front of me?*

I've replayed the scenario with wishfully crafted alternate endings. If only I could reverse time to the moment *just before* those girls started bullying my friend. I would stand up and demand, "Stop kicking my friend! Stop being mean! He's my friend!" And then Garrett and I would hug, and he'd know he was loved.

But I can't go back. And even if I could, I'd be eight years old again, consumed with panic, doubt, and fear about the consequences of calling out a crew of bullies. Unfortunately, I think my wishful self knows that my actual self would respond no differently.

THE BULLIED

Fast forward to middle school. One day I was briskly walking down the school hallway carrying my books and notebooks in my arms while my backpack uncomfortably dangled from one shoulder. Everyone knew it was *far* too uncool to wear a backpack fully strapped to both shoulders, and middle school Amy would have *never* chosen comfort over coolness or function over fashion.

As I walked by myself, I heard a few female voices quickly approaching behind me. Before I could turn around, Laura shoved me from behind. My books, notebooks, loose-leaf paper, and pens went flying and scattered across the hallway floor. People attempted to avoid stepping on my things while also craning their necks to see what was happening. A few even chanted, "Girl fight, girl fight!"

Laura was my mean girl. I genuinely had no idea why she hated me, but she made it abundantly clear that she did. She regularly found me in the hallways to say mean shit to me. This time, she was red in the face and shouting, "You're a fucking slut. Everyone thinks you're such hot shit, but you're not. You're a whore. I should just beat the shit out of you." She was flanked by two other girls who quietly encouraged her with head nods and comments like, "Yeah, you tell her," and "Mmhmm, that's right."

I desperately tried to ignore her verbal insults as I hurriedly picked up my stuff and scurried off through the crowd.

As I sat in my next class, I could barely think straight. My ears were buzzing, my heart was pounding, and my thoughts raced: *What did I ever do to deserve that? Why does she hate me so much? Why didn't anyone stop her? What the hell am I supposed to do now? I obviously can't tell a teacher. Will this ever end?*

I knew that telling a teacher would just result in worse mistreatment. Laura would get punished for bullying and then she'd double down on her efforts to harass me. I was certain the routine verbal bullying would turn into a physical altercation if I ratted her out.

When I returned home that afternoon, I explained the scenario to my mom and cried, "I don't understand what I ever did to make her hate me so much. I'm seriously scared that she's going to try to fight me."

My mom replied, "Honey, it's hard to say what she is going through. Just keep ignoring her. Hopefully she'll get bored and leave you alone."

I took my mom's advice and avoided my bully at all costs. I was relieved when she eventually stopped following me. I could only hope she didn't turn her aggression toward someone else. But at the same time, I thought, *phew, at least it wasn't me.* Ugh. I hate that I thought that.

THE BULLY

At 38 years old, I started dating the nicest guy I've ever dated. He was literally my next-door neighbor and ten years younger than me. We started hanging out regularly because we both loved deeply philosophical conversations, listening to good music, drinking wine, and eating good cheese. We ate other food, too. But we ate a lot of cheese.

We spent nearly every single night together hopping between his apartment and mine. We would joke about cutting a hole in the wall between our apartments so we could have easier access. He was a rule-follower, though, and was adamant that he didn't want to date anyone. So, there was obviously never going to be an *actual* doorway between our places.

Despite his professed desire to remain single, we spent every day together for months. Eventually, we started *officially* dating.

I'll admit that I really wanted the relationship to work even though I realized it wasn't ideal. We always had a great time hanging out, I loved his family, and my dogs adored him. However, he truly did not want to be in a committed relationship and was pretty sure he didn't foresee kids in his future.

I really wanted kids. I often thought, *why am I trying to make this work? Because, duh, he is the literal nicest guy I've ever dated.*

But here's the problem. My unmet need for a deeply committed relationship with someone who wanted to start having kids was causing resentment to build. I was 38 years old; it was time to get this kid-making show on the road.

While spending time with him felt fun, it also felt like a dead-end because he didn't want the things that truly mattered to me.

Here's where this story gets shitty.

I started being mean to him. Not all the time. Just when other stressors pushed my resentment and unconscious feelings of rejection over the edge.

Things would be going along just fine, and then the perfect storm of a long, stressful day and hunger would set the stage for deep feelings of rejection, disappointment, and fear. I felt rejected because he didn't want to be more committed. I was disappointed in myself for not prioritizing my relationship needs. I was afraid I'd never fulfill my dream of having children.

This toxic brew led to some shitty bullying behavior. Thankfully, I've now had a decade of therapy and reflection to realize how unkindly I treated him at my lowest points. One specific incident I deeply regret took place at a friend's wedding.

The night started with a shitstorm of self-criticism because I couldn't find anything to wear to the wedding. I looked in the mirror and thought, *I look like shit. I don't own enough Spanx to squeeze into anything cute. How the fuck do I weigh this much? Why haven't I taken better care of myself? I need to drink less wine and eat less cheese. Jesus, Amy, get your shit together.*

Rather than sharing these vulnerable feelings with my partner, I chose to overcompensate with feigned confidence. I settled on a black dress, a pair of sexy stilettos, and some bold jewelry that screamed *confidence!* I strutted out of my apartment as if all was well with me, and we drove to the wedding together.

At the wedding, I continued the internal self-judgment. My social anxiety had me thinking my friends wanted nothing to do with me. I critiqued everything that came out of my mouth: *Amy, seriously that was so stupid. Why did you say that? They're just laughing to humor you. These people couldn't care less if you were here. Jesus, Amy, just go get another drink.*

Drinking alcohol is helpful; it quiets my inner critic.

As the night progressed, everyone started moving to the dance floor. Our friend was the DJ so the music was excellent. I've danced my whole life and feel very confident on the dance floor. Dancing is my jam.

My brother was at the wedding, too. He's my favorite dance floor partner, especially when the DJ is playing 90s hip hop. As we danced to "Nuthin' But A G Thang" by Dr. Dre and Snoop Dogg, I finally felt settled into myself. I was being me. My feet hurt like hell because those fucking stilettos were a terrible choice. But other than that, I was feeling like my true self.

Then, my boyfriend joined us on the dance floor.

My inner critic, sore feet, the alcohol, and my unmet relationship needs collided. I became annoyed with his very presence. *How dare he—this person who doesn't really want me and definitely doesn't want kids with me—come out on this dance floor and interrupt a moment of blissful authenticity? How dare he try to steal away what little joy I've experienced tonight?*

As he danced with me, I started judging him harshly. I'm not proud of it, but I found a way to overcome my insecurities and shame: superiority. I'm a better dancer than him. I thought, *who cares if he rejects me, I'm too good for him anyway.* It's shitty that I had the thought, but what's worse is that I decided to displace my own shame by bringing the thought to life. And, I did it in an especially unkind way.

I said, "Dude, you dance like a white guy."

I watched him deflate.

I immediately regretted speaking that sentence. *What an asshole. Why did I say that?*

Because it's true.

Jesus, Amy. Now you're not only fat, but you're a rude, racist bully. Get your fucking life together.

When the song ended, my boyfriend left the dance floor. I danced with my brother and friends for the rest of the night. I acted as if I hadn't just bullied the nicest guy I'd ever dated. I knew I hurt him, didn't apologize, and pretended everything was fine.

We eventually broke up and I was devastated to lose the friendship. Unsurprisingly, he cited the wedding incident as one of the reasons he didn't feel respected or cared for. I apologized, but the damage was done. I hurt someone I deeply cared about because I was a bully.

THE WORST BULLY OF ALL

Eight-year-old me thought to herself, *Amy, you're a terrible friend. How could you sit by and let Garrett be bullied by those girls? You're horrible and unlovable.*

Middle school me thought, *what did you do to make her hate you? Obviously, you did something to deserve this. You're horrible and unlovable.*

Grown-up, 38-year-old me thought *you're a fat, miserable cow who insults nice guys when they're dancing with you. You're horrible and unlovable.*

Countless times throughout my life, I've bullied myself into believing I'm horrible and unlovable. I've told myself I'm lazy, stupid, unorganized, fat, unmotivated, unlikeable, unattractive, self-absorbed, and generally unworthy.

Why do we do this?

Why do we disparage, belittle, and bully ourselves?

Why do we posture as if we're not experiencing self-doubt and struggle?

Because we're taught to embrace unhealthy and unrealistic social standards.

We're taught to strive for perfectionism.

We're taught to judge, criticize, and shame others for not being perfect.

But we're also taught to be humble and minimize our own successes.

Rugged individualism is prized, yet the fear of rejection due to nonconformity is espoused.

Women are taught to minimize their needs in order to keep people happy.

We're taught that our worth is directly tied to our appearance.

We're taught that the worst thing we can be is fat.

We hustle for approval and forget who we are in the process.

THE PRACTICE

How do we return to our truest, most authentic selves when we're constantly listening to the world's demands through the critical voice of our inner bully?

We do something that is innately human.

We connect.

We connect with that inner bully and ask questions. Find out what's going on. What is it trying to tell you?

Maybe you've heard that you should "silence your inner critic." Or, that you should "shut that shit down." And maybe, like me, you've learned that drinking alcohol or staying crazy busy with work, social events, social media, and Netflix binges can distract you from your inner bully. But the bully is still there, and unlike my middle school bully, your inner bully will not suddenly go away because you're ignoring what it has to say.

Imagine if you were screaming at someone that they were fucking something up and they just tried to silence or ignore you? What would you do?

You'd get louder and more insistent. That's what happens with your inner bully. The more you try to silence it, the louder it gets. Instead of trying to quiet the bully, take the time to get to know it. What is it trying to teach you?

Over time, I've learned that mindfulness about my self-critical thoughts is key to my own healing. Not only does this lead to my own improved health and well-being, but I'm also more capable of showing up for others in supportive and loving ways. Rather than being subject to incessant internal bullying, I'm now listening attentively to the mean voice in my head. When my bully gets shitty with me, I listen. As it turns out, she's usually telling me something important, even if she's not doing it in a very nice way.

Generally, my inner bully gives me insight into my own fears, worries, insecurities, and shame. When I create space to hear what she is saying, the inner dialogue between my wise, centered self and my inner bully sounds a lot like a conversation between a grounded, kind, curious, and open-minded grown-up speaking with a dysregulated, petulant, hysterical child.

As the conversation between my wise self and my inner bully progresses, the bully calms down. By holding the space to hear what she's trying to say, I'm able to make sense of what's going on. As I inquire about the self-judgment and criticism, I'm able to reorient myself to my core values and move forward with value-aligned thoughts and actions.

The more mindfully I tend to my inner bully, the quieter and calmer she remains over time.

HOW TO TALK TO YOUR INNER BULLY

Cultivating a healthy relationship with my inner bully has taken me years of learning about mindfulness and developing a mindfulness practice. The principles of Acceptance Commitment Therapy (ACT) and Internal Family Systems (IFS) have helped me learn to override my programmed responses and numbing behaviors when my inner critic gets loud. With the help of skilled therapists and wisdom-guided friends, I've learned to tend to my self-judgment and criticism with curiosity, calmness, and wisdom.

My colleague and friend, Lisa Laughman, teaches emotional wellness and psychological resilience. In her six-part framework for tending to difficult emotions like self-criticism and shame, the first step is acknowledgement.

Here's where it gets real. Put down the glass of wine, turn off your binge-worthy show, log off social media, clear your harried schedule, and make space to accept that you've been desperately trying to ignore the shitty, self-critical thoughts your inner bully is slinging at you.

Acknowledge your inner bully. Say hello.

Give your bully some quiet space to share its thoughts. Get curious. Ask your bully why it's worried. Inquire about its concerns. Listen and ask questions. You'll be surprised how much you can learn about yourself when you stop numbing and start listening.

Not sure what to do next? Get support and learn how to develop a healthy relationship with your inner critic by joining the Bully-Free Future™ Mindset course on The Rebellion Community at therebellion.online. During the course, you will learn psychological flexibility skills, shame resilience tools, and the six-step framework for tending to difficult emotions. You will ultimately develop a practice of gratitude and mindfulness that will result in the discovery of who you are, what you really care about, and how you want to impact the world around you.

If you're ready to start creating a more emotionally balanced and bully-free future in your mind, come join us on *The Rebellion* for a holistic mindset experience that will truly change your life.

Amy M. Wisner, Ph.D., is audacious and unapologetic in her quest to dismantle oppressive systems by helping people become their most authentic selves. As a former rule-following good girl, she can deeply empathize with anyone who struggles to break the rules. Once upon a time, she wanted nothing more than to check the patriarchal life boxes, keep everyone happy, and live happily ever after.

After powering through the not-so-happily-ever-after, Amy chose a different path. At nearly 40 years old, she began a rebel journey of questioning the rules and discovering her truth within. Amy stopped coloring her gray hair, became a single mom by choice, and got a bunch of tattoos. She's now living her best life as Olivia and Caleb's mom, a professor at Michigan State University, and the founder of The Rebellion, a virtual community of rebels committed to creating a Bully-Free Future™ through authenticity, brave interactions, and anti-bully activism.

Amy is an interpersonal communication researcher, professor, and lifelong learner with a background in business and a deep need to understand human communication behavior. She researches social influence to understand how people create meaningful change.

Amy recently launched the RebelED Bully-Free Future™ (BFF) series on The Rebellion. Through this series of interactive courses, students master the BFF mindset, practice having brave conversations, and embark on anti-bully activism with the goal of creating a bully-free future for generations to come.

To learn more about Amy's rebel journey, check out her TEDxMSU talk. She discusses how patriarchy is disadvantaging women and men. She also shares her story of becoming a single mom by choice. Join The Rebellion and start creating a Bully-Free Future™ with one self-loving, authentic, kind, and compassionate act at a time.

Connect with Amy:

On The Rebellion: www.therebellion.online

Website: www.cancelthepatriarchy.org

Social media: https://linktr.ee/cancelthepatriarchy

"Put down the glass of wine, turn off your binge-worthy show, log off social media, clear your harried schedule, and make space to accept that you've been desperately trying to ignore the shitty, self-critical thoughts your inner bully is slinging at you."

~ Amy M. Wisner

Chapter 17

ANGELIC AWARENESS

MASTERING LOVE AS
A DIVINELY GUIDED SOUL

Patrick S. Fisher, Spiritual Coach

MY STORY

It was once an industrialized city full of well-paying factory jobs. Now the ghost city of Schenectady, New York, is a walking tomb for spiritual warfare and sightings. Driving through the decrepit city and looking through the window into the dimming night, I spotted a shadow figure darting across the busy intersection. Intuitively, I could feel it was the lost soul of a young, recently departed teenager. As I continued to wait for the light to change, I spotted what the young spirit was running from so desperately. Two larger demonic apparitions gave frantic chase, apparently trying to take this soul to wherever they came from.

As a psychic and intuitive empath, it's common for me to be able to see the war which rages with spiritual prowess. I instantly felt connected with this young soul and the notion of despair and hardship it was to endure was painstaking. As the red light changed green, I said a silent prayer: *Dear God, please rescue all souls in need, especially this young, tormented soul, and cast out the darkness from this world; amen.* In a world where creation is endlessly possible, faith and prayer are the supernaturally driven force to dispel the low vibrational forces which try to drag us downwards.

Just as despair began to fill my inner being, a magnificent light from above caught my attention. The sky was illuminated by this beautiful, angelic being floating in magnificent glory. The angel, dressed perfectly for battle, had on blaze gold armor, long golden hair, and held a sword in hand. The angel's light gave off the most mesmerizing white glow, which literally illuminated all around him. The color of this white illumination was beyond the white color schemes we see in our world. The warrior angel looked like Michael the Archangel, and I suspect it probably was. As I stared in humbling awe, the angel pointed its sword straight up, then shot up in the air with this powerful, illuminating light. I could only make out its light as the angel traversed the sky, flying in a fantastical motion that reminded me of God's word, "Let there be light." The heavenly angel flew deep into the tree line, heading into battle and bringing hope again into my night.

We all seek to be loved and understood in life. However, my childhood taught me that as a lightworker, I had to be the "way-shower" to those of my kin that lack an openness to connect with the spirit world around us. Walking away from those who hurt me for a lifetime was not an easy task. I went through a divorce, dealt with surgery and health issues, and knew that none of them could help me with the path I was on.

As I packed what little possessions I took from the breakup, I felt terrible sadness and isolation beyond what I care to explain in words. I cried for the first time in years and sat in a place of discomfort. Alone, I drove to the National Cemetery and sat in deep, meditative contemplation. It was crucial to see the graves around me of those who were deceased. I thought to myself: *There's my cousin Chad Burns' grave right over in row seven. He was an Army Combat, Purple Heart, Iraq war veteran, and here he rests after passing away so young. I cannot just sit here and quit. I must get up and move forward with my life. This is not the end for me. Not here, not now. They are resting in peace, but I still have things I need to achieve in my life.*

Heading back home for the third visit to the Cemetery, I told myself, "Everything is going to be alright, Patrick; God has you." As I lay down to sleep that night, I began a spiritual transformation that can only aptly be described as going through death and rebirth. Crying out in agony throughout the night, actual burns began to show up across my chest and even left a red line underneath. As I moaned in discomfort, it felt like I was burning away the old aspects that no longer aligned with my life and purpose. This new journey is all about self-love and mastering the art of positive vibrational energies!

As I made it through the ego death described above, others began noticing the psychical transformation in me. This transformation was drastic, fast, and shocking to some people I hadn't reconnected with in years. Behind the scenes, it felt like these angels were taking away all the pain from my heart. It felt like they were spiritually operating on me in my sleep, and the marks were the remnants of the changes going on with me.

My interests began to shift, and my calling was from God himself. I had no idea about the immense transformation the Lord had ready for me. Sitting alone in my apartment, I thought: *Why do those who are supposed to love us act so ruthlessly in their inability to love?* It made me sad, but then my departed grandmother, Rose, came through. She is always a powerful intercessor with God and steers souls back toward his grace. My grandmother was the driving force in many people's lives, a subtle matriarch filled with divine love and wisdom. As I sat there meditating, the memory came through of her passing. My world felt like it was truly shattered. The one person I could call and tell of my spiritual encounters was now passed on. I worked for the government then, building weapons of war I didn't wish to be a part of. Her death made that notion paramount in my drive to change. I picked up the phone and dialed my work.

"Hello," my boss answered. "Hello, Sir, this is Patrick Fisher," I responded.

"I feel like I'm having a mental breakdown doing this type of work."

I went on. "I just no longer want to contribute to producing weapons that are used to hurt other human beings."

"I see; I'm sorry to hear that. I hope you're seeking help. Please stop by next week so you may turn in your government badge," he replied. Clearly, this was not the first time he had had this conversation with others.

"Thank you for the opportunity, Sir," was all I said.

I got into my car and began heading into town away from my hurting heart. A vision engulfed my mind as I drove the green, pastured country roads. It felt like I was dreaming yet still awake. I began to see images of Jesus in the most vivid colored green grass. His smile lit up at me like his joy was the echo of vibrational love. We began walking together and talking like old friends would on a stroll through a peaceful landscape. This image was so powerful in my mind that I had to pull the car off the country road. I could no longer drive but rather cried like a baby. I knew my grandmother was showing me that she was with Jesus, and I prayed for him to go visit her personally as a direct favor to me. I knew this would mean everything to her, so naturally, it was everything I could ask of God. The perfect gift for the humble matriarch who always showered me with unconditional love and support.

The military is a place that is by the books, with standards and orders for everything a soldier or sailor will do while in service. Faith is sort of an abstract thought that tends to come into play during times of hardship, death, and turmoil. It's like something you keep to yourself until the moment of total breakdown when you need something to believe in. Returning from deployment, I was at an all-time low regarding my transition back to stateside life. I began to become depressed and isolated and had a horrible time trying to sleep. The nightmares of the traumatic events haunt me like a horrid compulsion in the night.

When others would call their home safety and comfort, my Washington D.C. apartment became like living in Hell on Earth. The more depressed I got, the lower my vibrations were, and the less faith I had to rely upon. One night this horrible apparition came out of my closet, which caused me to flee in repulsion. As I lay in bed with my dog at my feet, a ten-foot, blacker-than-black, hunched-over figure appeared in robes—a terrifying sight. The figure came to the foot of my bed as I stared in fright from the initial shock. The figure looked like the classic depiction of death and reached out its putrid-smelling arm and grabbed my feet. I jumped up in a powerful motion and fled out of my bedroom and into the living room. Night after night, this demonic figure entered through the portal in my closet and into my place of sanctity.

I called my grandmother crying that first night. "Hello, Patrick; how are you, sweetheart?" She asked with motherly concern.

"Hi Gram, I have to tell you about this demon that is terrifying me!" I cried out in pain. She listened intently and said she'd call my uncle to ask for advice. Of course, she also said she would pray for me. The next day she returned my call after speaking with him.

"Put up the picture of the Sacred Heart of Jesus," she said. "That is his loving promise and sacrifice he gave to this world and to you," she went on.

Following this advice, I went to a store and purchased the picture she recommended. The power of this picture would rock the very essence of what that demonic menace was made of. I placed the picture in my room, directly above my bed. Now, if you asked me what a demon is, I'd reply that they're a coward bred upon evil that seeks only to do cowardly acts to those at their very lowest in life. That night, I discovered that the demon became trapped outside of my bedroom, fleeing from the promise of God's beloved son, The Prince of Peace. It became so enraged that as I lit a candle in my room, instinctively, I felt the need to check the bathroom. As I went inside, the candle burst like fire and shrapnel all over my bedroom. It was such a shocking sound that it took me a brave moment to open the door and see the mess that ensued.

Next, as I walked into the hallway, the demon began shoving me repeatedly in the back, harder than a human being could push me. I eventually had enough, walked into my room, and slammed the door very hard in the demon's face. That night, the entity took it a step further as I went in to take a shower. This demonic force turned on all the burners on my stove and filled my apartment with gas. Eventually, the handyman on duty, Willy, busted through my door to investigate the gas leak.

This event shocked me and left me feeling extremely angry at my circumstances. I couldn't just go to my superiors and tell them what I was experiencing. Instead, I had to become the spiritual warrior that I am. Lighting up a full box of incense, I sat in the living room alone with the Bible. The demon could not stand the purifying smell, which taught me a simple rule in dealing with these entities. "Cleanliness is close to Godliness." This saying meant the world to me at that moment. I opened the Bible and began to read verses out loud. I could feel my angels come to my aid and guide me through what I needed to do. I began speaking in a pure, Irish accent while channeling the wisdom and reciting the words with my guardian angel, David Mchennary. He is my great-great-grandfather and was a remarkable man of faith. David showed me that evening that the very same light which flows in angels is the same light that flows from our soul. The demon fled in pure terror as I began my own journey to the realization of my own spiritual powers and authority.

Seeing the purity in my own child, Rowan, has led me to take great strides of inner healing. Learning and researching spirituality has led me to want to be a love-filled beacon of light in her life and for the world. The same empathy, compassion, love, and strength in me also run through her in the same spiritual gifts. Just as there is darkness in this world, so too is there light. Learning to master our environment and making it a temple of safety and love allows us to attract angelic assistance. As we become Earth angels, the demonic forces wish to steer us off our path. Just in writing this chapter, I've been spiritually attacked on a harsh level for the past week. This led to terrible pain from passing a kidney stone. Small price to pay for assisting others on their path to enlightenment. However, I'm always divinely protected, and these attacks just leave me tired or drained. Divine healing allows me to transmute hateful energies and to lead as an empowered, loving soul.

THE PRACTICE

Life lessons led me to teach that to live as an example of love, we must move past the hurt of the past. Taking time to heal, embracing faith in God, and seeing the angelic signs lead to greater spiritual awareness, allowing you to see the world from a unique lens while gaining valuable wisdom and insight.

Taking time to burn candles and incense, and to keep icons of God and your beliefs, allows you to live in a home free of malevolent spirits hell-bent on evil. Seeing and embracing the signs from your angels and deceased loved ones should instill a greater sense of faith in you. If you see these messages in things like red cardinals, butterflies, coins, radio music, messages, billboards, and numerology signs, start paying attention to the impressions and feelings it brings to you. Start asking your angels to help show themselves to you. Be open to your dreams and the messages of change that come forth. Be brave in making these changes while striving to attune your energies to the angelic realm. When you're in a low vibration or depressed, the angel's presence can become triggering for you to be in. Their love is so pure that it's a reminder to your higher self's soul of the work and changes you need to make. However, in making these changes, you may work alongside the angelic realm to help others heal and feel safe and uplifted on their own spiritual journeys while incarnated here.

My spiritual practice is centered around attracting angelic assistance. Here's some astounding secrets of my personal success to mastering the art of love.

Serving as an Earth angel, you must be willing to operate out of a place of love. The meaning of life is love, so to become love, we must embrace the energy of love.

Examples of affirmations to recite daily:

"I am a loving, kind, spiritual being attracting the energy of love."

"I am centering my heart space with an openness to accept love, including the journey of self-love."

"I am serving the world as an angelic beam of light."

"I welcome the help of the angelic realm and seek to serve the world as a temple of light."

Making your living environment your temple of peace is love. Hanging up images of spiritual/religious icons of love help to promote a protected home. I recommend making your home an example of your artistic and decorative abilities centered on cleanliness and positive energy flow. Taking the time to recite prayers and loving words attracts the assistance and attention of higher-dimensional, loving support. Another way to protect your home and family is to allocate wind chimes, bells, and gongs to be an instrument that brings positive energies into your environment.

Furthermore, I suggest burning incense daily to keep your sanctuary free of lower-level energies. Just as the home needs to be cleansed, so too must we make time to keep our own energies in synch with love.

As we rise spiritually, we must also humble ourselves with the servitude of others. Doing positive deeds and sending love to those struggling is a true example of a divinely inspired leader. Taking "spiritual baths" with relaxing music is a wonderful example for a cleanse. I personally use rose water, lavender, and healing crystals directly in the bath itself. This allows tremendous amounts of the release of energies back into the water.

Another example of purification is taking a clean glass of water and placing it beneath your bed at night, then tossing the water out of your home back into the earth in the morning. This will help in bringing purification to any bad dreams.

Beyond the affirmations and purifications, we must also practice the art of self-love. Have you placed yourself first lately? Or ever, for that matter? If not, here is that divine moment of chance in life for you to truly love yourself for the beautiful essence of your God-given soul. Look in that mirror and tell yourself you are amazing and worthy of God's intentions for you today. Take that time to walk in nature, sit by that stream, and heal by the ocean. Each moment of God's radiance is a chance to master the art of love. This love is a divine promise to your soul to earn your peace while healing and release from past wounds are worth the journey of self-love.

Patrick S. Fisher, Spiritual Coach, is a source for healing and inspiration for coaching clients. After a decade of work with the Armed Forces and U.S. Government, Patrick attended SUNY Adirondack College, followed by Siena College with an English Major and Religious Studies Minor. He is now pursuing a degree in psychology from Southern New Hampshire University. With this degree, Patrick plans on pursuing studies at the Newton Institute and helping clients through therapy and past life regression. He found himself through deep meditation, cultural studies, and an openness to come out spiritually to share his gifts with the world.

After launching a successful life coaching business and blog, Patrick began using his spiritual gifts of healing, clairvoyance, clairaudience, and discernment to help clients find answers. With over a decade of experience in biblical studies, numerology, astrology, and tarot, Patrick has found that combining spirituality and self-love is key to transformation. He creates short stories, writes on spiritual topics, and is an activist for promoting change and ascending to a more loving world.

Patrick can channel wisdom and guidance from the higher realms to guide clients. Setting a clear vision, he helps clients to find their inner voice and to set meaningful goals every step of their personal journey.

He is a visionary in his peaceful approach, allowing clients to truly open up and find those hidden talents and passions that change the trajectory of life.

Connect with Patrick:

Website: Spiritual Healing and Self-love guidance – Spiritual Blog (wordpress.com)Patrickfisher333.wordpress.com

E-mail: Ps12fish@icloud.com

Links to Social Media:

Facebook: https://www.facebook.com/profile.php?id=100079704319414

LinkedIn: http://linkedin.com/in/patrick-fisher-love-is-the-meaning-of-life-blessed-055574180

Instagram: @Patrickfisher1234

TikTok: @Patrickfisher243

"Just as despair began to fill my inner being, a magnificent light from above caught my attention. The light was being illuminated off of this beautiful, angelic being floating in the sky in magnificent glory."

~ Patrick S. Fisher

Chapter 18

WEATHERING LIFE'S STORMS

GETTING BACK ON TRACK WITH EASE

Frank Byrum

MY STORY

I sat down in my chair and strained to reach around the boulder on my lap. No matter how hard I tried, my arms seemed too short. The keyboard was frozen just beyond reach, and the blinking cursor was a siren calling me to work.

It was as if the cursor continued to mock me, telling me everything the drive-by emotional vampire said was true.

I was frozen, unable to move—frozen to the depths of my soul.

Another day, unable to focus, unable to work, unable to function.

The boulder, a hallway encounter, an emotional dump, misdirected anger from the boss, again.

Picking up the broken pieces of my psyche, trying to gather my emotions, I crawled back to my office, led the video call, and tried to work.

Ever carried an emotional boulder?

Unlike Sisyphus, I hadn't cheated death, and still, somehow, a childhood pebble became an enormous rock, now my gargantuan boulder in a life that seemed laborious and futile.

Maybe it's the argument with your spouse before work. Or the boss stomped you down again. Or a co-worker stabbed you in the back. Or maybe it's an insufferable parent that has never been pleased.

It's the inexplicable backache in the morning, the daily migraines at night.

The endless brain loops that repeat over and over and over—at 3 a.m. They haunt your dreams, and after scant sleep, they repeat during morning coffee.

Every time you gather the strength to push forward, moments later, the brain-loop steps in to remind you of every jot and tittle, every detail of everything that ever went wrong, and those who called you out for the smallest infraction.

Sometimes it's the words said to me, those knives that cut to the bone.

Sometimes it's the words I wanted to say but was never brave enough.

Sometimes it's the escape plan—to run away, so detailed and specific, it's hard to wonder why I never left.

Sometimes it's all these and more—over and over and over again.

And meditation was the worst; the brain-loop goes into megaphone mode at full volume—at eleven.

And day after day, I shoulder my Sisyphus boulder. It was endless, and I imagined it would go on longer than an eternity.

I blamed myself and my parents, and my relationships. I felt it must be the workload, the traffic, or the dog. It was everything, or it felt like everything.

I thought by 30, I'd get my life together, and I'd get my "shit in one sock." I ran hard and tried to please everyone except myself and do all things except my own desires.

By 40, I figured, maybe I was a late bloomer, and later that decade, facing a divorce only added to the brain loops: the internal negative narrative and resentment.

When 50 came around, cynicism replaced optimism, and I realized I had lived a facade. In vulnerable moments, most, if not all those I knew confessed they had or were deeply struggling. Each of them had boulders that were part of their own making, part from childhood, and from many hardships, disappointments, and abuses—and all of them shouldering a daily boulder up the mountain over and over again.

I saw many loved ones fall into a cycle of dude-bro sports, hunting, or partying addictions. Others were spending into credit-card prison, in perpetual debt many times their incomes. Others were having emotional affairs on social media, a few living the secrets of infidelity, and many were echoing the far left or far right rhetoric with such anger and venom they destroyed long-term friendships and family.

In my estimation, all were trying to assuage the emotional struggles to continue to keep going every day. And I noticed that if each had not done at least the initial hard work of internal healing before 40, the internal demons seemed to permanently change these once kind and loving humans into Jekyll and Hyde. These tried to hide their struggles, and by their mid-60s, nearing retirement, the masks were so full of cracks that it was impossible to cover up the truth.

To be honest, I had a propensity to accept the emotional vampires, the overt and covert narcissists, and their never-ending cycle of love bombing, emotional dumping, and self-aggrandizing.

My karma drew these people into my life, and along with my childhood insecurities, left me trying to help everyone be okay so I could also be okay. That turned into an endless "yes" and pleasing everyone except myself. In times of stress, I became a workaholic to attempt to earn a modicum of approval.

For decades, I lost myself and didn't even know who I was or what I desired.

Early in my separation, I went out alone to eat at a "favorite" restaurant and ordered my standard meal. After I took a bite, I thought, *I fucking hate this food and this place.*

I have lived on auto-pleasing for so long that I had no idea who I was.

I certainly didn't "know myself" even though I knew my feelings had been pushed down repeatedly; my desires remained unexpressed and unmet.

Looking back, I can see how often the same narrative unfolded, and I fell into the loop, a black hole trap that left me always trying to please, never allowing even a modicum of happiness to sustain.

Over the years, I learned to say, "Oh, that's just so and so," and struggled to "turn the other cheek." It's oddly funny to realize the slaps to my face continued until, in frustration, I decided to end the relationship. Then the "narcissistic friend" turned into a victim and badmouthed me again and again.

Over time, I didn't need the narcissist's word spells anymore; my brain loops took over the job for them. Even after establishing boundaries and ending relationships, I still struggled deeply, trying to break the spell, let go of the words, and trust my own intuition.

After decades, the boulder grew larger. I struggled to function and lived a secret life of perpetual resentment and anger.

"Damnit, why can't I reach this keyboard? If I don't get working soon, I will get further behind and lose this job."

I had friggin' work to do, and if the feeling of being behind wasn't enough, the difficulty of staring at that emotional boulder was crushing.

It seemed Hades sentenced me, or maybe I was paying down past Karma—rolling a daily boulder up every grueling mountain. The irony is that I've always been able to step away from behind the boulder and leave it behind. Unconsciously - that is, unaware - I always shouldered, or rather chose, the burden.

I was willing to serve a prison sentence for crimes I didn't commit or understand. When really the prison door had always been open, all brain loops and beliefs were self-imposed. I could've been free at any moment.

Initially, I threw myself into my family's religion, becoming an uber-good guy. While I believe all traditions teach valuable guidelines for life, I didn't want to be so good as to be free of the endless rules and expectations.

Oddly, it took decades to go deep enough to see how at an early age, all this began—around five or so. I had fallen into the loops so young as not to realize.

Laughing out loud. Now I know I was free all along and yet was so domesticated and trained and in fear, I kept shouldering the emotional boulder and rolling it up the exponential mountain. Along the way, I learned to emotionally self-abuse and blame myself, and the days turned into years and then into decades.

I struggled to admit it to my closest friend: myself!

I could never admit it to my close friends or family.

If you are there, you likely have a similar story. And you've embraced your own boulder, and you're pushing it up your own mountain.

It's a secret life—wake up, paint on a happy face, and muse again—as I allow the current narcissist to dismantle my self-worth, self-image, and self-love.

While the Oracle of Delphi was saying, "Know Thyself," all I could do was listen to the Oracles of Narcissism, "you're worthless."

Believing, I fell into the self-help loop: books, videos, and podcasts. Don't get me wrong, many of these contained the critical tools and techniques I so deeply needed; I just couldn't break free.

Even though many devoted mentors and coaches lovingly told me the truth and though I learned the tools, walk, and talk, I still struggled to defend long abandoned borders and to maintain boundaries.

Each day, pressing against the boulder—often running in place, restless and ever diligent, saying: "Just one more act, one more duty, and they will come around and acknowledge my worth; and I could earn it all back and be free."

On a few occasions, I thought this was true until the word spells brought the boulder, pushing me further into the valley.

My emotional bank was empty and overdrawn.

If you've been there, your emotional bank account will be overdrawn again and again, to zero and below. Each overdraft is a new low and somehow, after reaching the bottom, just like Dante's Hell, there are many levels below.

Like you, I had my escapes: a fast-food lunch, an extra glass of wine, and doom-scrolling. I tried hobbies, religion, and workaholism.

For decades, it was just enough until it wasn't. It was years of being bowled over and crashes and new lows, and no one knew; I hid it all. I can't say that anyone ever knew, and I was too afraid to admit my inner struggle to anyone—even in prayer to God. Since I'm writing this chapter, somehow, I was able to escape or at least receive enough light to step into freedom.

It was when I started to look deep inside, listen to my inner voice, and learn that my intuition could be trusted that I began the journey to freedom. Over the decades, I made nominal progress and began letting go, and then under stressful circumstances, picked up the boulder again and started pushing.

I finally realized this is my default mode and that I'd have to move from a *passive* to an *active* awareness to reach anything that resembles freedom.

Over time, I tested tools and techniques and developed a practice, my personal daily practice, that brought me to the truth, awareness, and strength necessary to change. There were many experiments and failures, and whenever I thought things were under control, I fell again.

The Grandmaster said, "Fall down seven, get up eight."

In short, I kept getting up, even after each battle seemed lost.

Ultimately, I found the critical key: **Awareness!**

When I allowed myself the honesty of my own feelings and emotions and began to be aware and accept each as information, and information in conjunction with my intuition, I learned to navigate toward longer periods of freedom.

Awareness is all that's necessary, especially if that awareness reveals the truth. At the earliest point of awareness is the point to choose differently. And in the end, I had to be willing to lose it all and walk away from everything, and start again with nothing. I was so sick and tired of it all—it was a life-and-death choice.

There are times in life when you must push through, even after awakening and realizing it's all wrong. As in a story where the princess is awakening from a spell, an illusion. Daily practice is the key to *peeling the onion* of emotional vampires' word spells and walking away with the power of awareness and intuition to freedom.

It was the deep introspection that came through my daily practice and the self-knowledge revealed that turned into the awareness in the moment—the awareness required to break the default old decision loops and, with bravery and faith, allowed me to make different choices. This is truly waking up from surviving a living-death into a living-life.

This is the art I practice and teach, to develop a daily practice and to discover yourself, your authentic and true self, and without fear or apology, learn to live your life.

I'm not saying my struggles are over or that I've come to enlightenment; what I'm saying, and maybe promising, is that you can move forward and learn to breathe again by beginning this journey.

And you, too, can develop a daily practice that'll sustain you during hard times and will be instrumental in awakening your own meditation awareness and intuition practice—your path to freedom. Remember, life is a journey, life will change, and there will always be challenges. And you can also learn to exercise your freedom and choose; and learn to live life abundantly, more under your own terms than those dictated by others, especially your long-term emotional brain loops and the vampiric word spells that are not serving you very well.

This is what I'm offering—a simple daily practice that is the initial step toward awareness. It seems too simple, and yet you will find this powerful tool is both the door key and the escape passage to a new life.

I learned from my mentor, a martial arts Grandmaster, that it isn't that I should acquire more techniques and tools; it's that I must minimize my toolbox, learn to master a few and discover my power.

You, too, can begin to know yourself and get back on track with ease, weathering life's storms and, in awareness, embrace your intuition.

THE PRACTICE

Select a quiet place and give yourself time: I recommend having no activity planned for at least 30 minutes. When initially starting, it's important not to be emotionally rushed by your next activity.

In my practice, I brew a small pot of tea, bring a pen and writing pad, and sit outside, away from distractions.

The secret is the *tea* or *coffee* or a cue. Over time, it will become an internal reminder to your soul that you're about to enter your practice. This is essential to take your practice beyond your morning meditation and into the day.

Every time I need to re-sync, after a difficult phone conversation or before an important meeting, or to escape, I get a cup of tea and take a few minutes, essentially the beginning of the practice below and breathe at least three or five times. This will heighten your awareness and allow your observer to hear your emotions, engage logic and intuition, and break the brain loop.

The tea-cue is what I use to engage my own internal grounding, focus inward, and shift my perspective out of my head and into the moment: it's a mindfulness meditation practice. I always have a teabag in my briefcase, at my desk, and in my car, and nearly every home, office, or nearby-coffee shop will do in a pinch.

To establish a daily practice, pick a set time daily. I generally wake very early and sit outside in nature if the weather permits. As fall approaches, it's very dark and quiet at first light. Find the quietest place possible, in nature, a park, or a quiet room. Use noise-canceling headsets as a last resort.

For the first few moments, just breathe normally without any rush. If your mind is chattering, write the thought or to-do on the pad.

Next, breathe deeply, filling the lungs from the bottom of the belly slowly to the top.

Slowly breathe deeply to a count of five or more and then slowly exhale. Allow the exhale count to be a few seconds longer than the inhale count.

It's normal for brain loops and chatter to appear. Get deeply curious. Don't fret, don't resist, embrace the chatter: today's to-do list, meetings, memories, anger, anything. Give yourself permission to attend to these later and write each on the pad as they appear. The pad is a parking lot for thoughts, a safe place where nothing will be lost or go unattended, and to help your mind let go for a time.

After a few minutes of breathing, place one or both of your hands on your heart.

Continue the breathing. Listen, just sit, and listen. Observe your thoughts and let each come.

What is my brain loop telling me?

Often what was on my mind before bed or what woke me at 3 am is still looping at 6 am the next morning.

Give yourself permission to fully feel any emotion, even if you have never allowed it before. With your hands on your heart, ask:

What is this telling me? What do I need to know?

Use your intuition and listen to what your soul already knows, and what in the past you have suppressed or resisted or what you don't want to face.

Listen and keep breathing; give yourself space, and time to be still and listen *and know.*

You may notice a deep feeling or a presence or hear a loving word or a whispered phrase of your younger self; sometimes at others, it may be a frustration or stern tenor.

These are inner parts, often stranded in the past, wanting to be heard. Get curious!

Write it down on your pad or in a journal. Even if it's horrible or ugly, you can hide it, burn it, or shred it later.

Listen without judgment and offer gratitude for any response.

Say a *thank you* for each insight or answer.

Breathe a few additional cycles and offer a prayer of gratitude. Write down your feelings, message, or experience in your journal.

Make this your daily practice and realize it may take a few sessions to begin to truly understand your brain loops. I've done this for decades, and over those years, my awareness has grown. I've learned to trust my daily practice, which ultimately led me to trust my intuition.

I often end my practice with a short wisdom lesson or an inspirational poem.

The goal is simple: to become fully attentive and aware of yourself and to listen. Remember, everything is information and once you begin to see the brain loops and word spells as just information, then you can engage other tools, especially intuition, to navigate the day.

There is no rush. This is your journey, and it took years to get here.

You are an amazing, brave soul for taking this first step and beginning your daily practice. Join me on my blog for additional resources and steps.

Be graceful, patient, and compassionate to yourself. Your soul has waited a lifetime for you to become aware and trust your inner knowing, your intuition.

Frank Byrum is a scientist, technologist, and best-selling author who has spent the last four decades on a spiritual journey, the last few of which have been focused on deep self-healing. His dad led his early spiritual training in the Southern Baptist tradition, and following in his footsteps for several decades, he continued the family tradition as a Bible teacher.

To continue his religious education, he began a Master of Theology in Apologetics, and it was during this time that he began to consider the teachings deeply and realized few taught or even mimicked Jesus' love, kindness, and healing. Ultimately not completing the degree and with this soul-belief—what was once known and practiced has been lost.

This questioning, this crisis of faith, led to decades of searching various wisdom traditions and teachers, and with a simple faith believing the promise of Mathew 7:7— "Ask, and it shall be given you; seek, and ye shall find; knock, and it shall be opened unto you" (KJV).

For years, he has shared his understanding with friends, family, students, and associates as he continued to research and practice. He earnestly believes everyone can benefit from the foundation of practical daily practice, and it's the best way to "be in the world, but not of the world." Today, his daily practice includes tea, breath work, prayer and meditation, martial arts katas, Qi-Gong energy work, and wisdom studies. He resides in southern Virginia, where he practices, teaches and writes.

Download a PDF of the exercise and a guided audio:
https://themindfulpathway.com

Connect with Frank:

Website: themindfulpathway.com

Email: frank@themindfulpathway.com

Twitter: https://twitter.com/MindfulPathway or @MindfulPathway

Instagram: https://www.instagram.com/tfbyrum

*"When I allowed myself the honesty of my own feelings
and emotions and began to be aware and to accept each as
information, and this information in conjunction with my
intuition, I learned to navigate toward longer periods of
freedom."*

~ Frank Byrum

Chapter 19

LIVING INSIDE OUT IN THE SECOND HALF

GETTING COMFORTABLE WITH DISCOMFORT

Jennifer Sproul, Realtor, Founder Graceing Agefully™

MY STORY

DATELINE: BEGINNING OF SCHOOL YEAR, 1970; REDDING, CONNECTICUT.

"Where will you be in life in the year 2000? We are approaching a new century and a new millennium." Mr. Cruson lobs the question to a roomful of half-awake 15- and 16-year-old anthropology students. I'm daydreaming, "Wait, what was the question?" I say under my breath.

He repeats and rephrases as he detects a shift in awareness in his young audience. "In the not too distant future, it will be a new century *and* a new millennium. What do you think your life will be like in the year 2000?"

I calculate quickly in my head (2000-1954)=46. Whoa, that's old!

I picture myself driving a station wagon, kids of assorted ages bouncing around in the seats. I'm dropping them off or picking them up—taxi service. I live in a large comfortable home in the Connecticut suburbs (just like I did then). I have a handsome husband who adores me and he's working hard to support us.

Again, in my head: *Wow, how did I get there? I've only been on one or two dates with boys alone. I can't imagine marrying them! What happens in between?*

Suddenly I've skipped past all the fun of school and boyfriends and I'm old, married, and responsible. It *seems* very far away. *What will happen between now and then?*

DATELINE: OCT. 31, 1999, PARIS, FRANCE

Raymond says, clearly aggravated, "Tonight, we are going to the Eiffel Tower!" It's not a request this time. It's our last night in Paris; we've been here for a week. I've been working all week, out to the factory outside Paris during the day, returning in the evening with an obligation to meet colleagues or an excuse not to do more than have a quiet dinner and turn in. After all, this is not *my* first time in Paris, but it *is* his. We did have one night, my birthday, earlier in the week, we recall fondly. We had an amazing, romantic, delicious, perfect dinner to celebrate my 45th birthday. We agreed; it was pure bliss—service like we had never experienced. Flickering, soft candlelight, sitting side by side on a loveseat at a corner table, amazing Bordeaux opened 30 minutes before reaching us to achieve perfect aeration before the first sip. A cart glides to our table boasting a perfectly prepared whole dorado (fish). Without a word, the waiter deftly filets and plates my entree, placing it before me and spiriting away upon noting our purrs of approval. This night is for *us*.

But, tonight is for us and particularly for Raymond. It's his first trip to Paris and probably my 12th in four years, most of them in the past year. My business travel with my French employer has allowed me to see parts of Europe I had never seen: Paris, Geneva, Edinburgh, London, Copenhagen, Nice, Monte Carlo, and Lake Annecy in the French Alps. Even better than that, on their dime.

I've saved the Eiffel Tower for Raymond, my boyfriend of five years, with whom I live back in Maryland. It seems only right that I save one of the most romantic tourist attractions for him. Now, it's our last night in Paris and we still haven't boarded the elevator to the top.

"Of course, let's go!" I say, knowing deep down he has something important in mind. Tremors in my gut, a solid lump forming in my throat, we set out for the short taxi ride to the other side of the Seine, Le Rive Droite. We return engaged.

DATELINE: JANUARY 1, 2000, ROCKVILLE, MARYLAND.

What I imagined at 15 was going to be my life in 2000 hadn't happened. Not even close. I wasn't married, never had been. I had no children.

So, was I **over?** Was I a failure?

When I reflect on the first 46 years of my life I recall a sense of striving. I always compared myself to my older siblings, stars, models, friends, and colleagues. Tomorrow, next week, next year, more and better was always just out of reach. I never quite measured up to what I thought were my expectations.

It was like I had been running miles on a treadmill and getting nowhere. I was racking up miles but had nothing to show. Nothing to show, if the external world was my ruler. My goals and measures of success in life were set by family, friends, society, culture, everyone, and everything but *me*.

By the year 2000, I reached what my 15-year-old self thought was old. I was also none of those things I envisioned at 15. I wasn't married. I had no children. That was big. Those two metrics were the objects of a conscious expectation throughout my life to that point. On that scale, I was not enough, at least in my mind, and I thought, also in the minds of others, my family, and even friends.

I was born at the tail end of the "women go to college to get an Mrs. degree" era (cringeworthy, isn't it?). That idea was embedded, however deeply hidden, in my subconscious.

In my 50s I could see my life wasn't going to look like anyone else's. I realized that for every perceived *failure* on the report card issued by external teachers, there was an equal or greater win on my *internal report card.*

For example, I had a career that took me all over Europe, taught me another language, introduced me to friends from other cultures, and gave me experiences I couldn't have afforded on my own. I was paid well, traveled first class, wined, and dined. I was self-sufficient and independent. I was happy.

I remember my mother in her late fifties, unhappy in her marriage and feeling trapped by financial insecurity. She felt she wasn't worthy or able to earn a living on her own because she devoted her youth to raising a family. That's what you did. She married the handsome pilot—he was smart, funny, and loved her. They had five children, who she more or less single-handedly raised while he was at war or flying. She never earned a living as an RN, although she finished nursing school. I recall thinking, *I don't want that to be **my** story.*

The individual forming in the first half of my life was a unique and wonderful creation. I know now that I was driven by a muffled inner voice. I was silencing that voice; she was screaming as if trapped in a soundproof room that I constructed to keep her quiet. Every once in a while, the door would crack open and I'd hear her. I'd shut the door again because she didn't meet what I thought were *my* expectations.

At 61 I concluded I could live to 125, maybe more. My parents outlived their parents by 30 years. They each lived to 94 and 99. With modern medicine and lifestyle modifications, I don't think that's a crazy idea.

My mindset shift occurred when I thought, *I'm only halfway. I have as many years ahead as I have already lived.* Today, I'm healthier physically and mentally than I was at 46. I'm still working, on my terms, I'm financially independent, and I see no reason to believe that I cannot continue to grow, earn, and learn indefinitely.

My inner voice was breaking through. I spent 60 years pursuing external ideals. I spent 60 years comparing myself to my expectations and giving myself a low grade. I spent 60 years avoiding *my* feelings, and 60 years not speaking up. My mindset of comparing and falling short brought me to an age I thought was too late to get it right. Then, the realization that I might be only halfway.

Now I'm listening deeply to that inner voice. In the second half, I'm living "inside out." For the first half, I lived "outside in." My aspirations were defined by external factors I thought were mine. They were not. Now, I'm guided by that inner voice, the inner guide; call it whatever works for you. . . God, angels, higher power (HP), and higher self are all involved.

My inner voice is no longer in a soundproof room. I'm tearing down the walls to hear her better. She assures me my life is perfect as is and is convincing me. She wants me to live every day with that in mind. She wants me to know that I am enough.

This is my **mindset** in the second half of my life. Although I am *enough* today, I'm not finished. I will continue to expand, grow, learn, and live more. As they say, "life is a journey, not a destination."

After my epiphany, I started surveying people around me, many of whom were already in their 70s. I asked them, "What if you learned from an unimpeachable source that you will live to be at least 100? What would you do differently?"

I thought they'd think for a minute, look a little mystified, and maybe say, "I'm not sure, I never looked at it that way." I thought, like me, they'd calculate and think, *30 years is a pretty long time; I feel pretty good today; I am going to give that some thought.*

Without exception, the responses were quick and decisive. With a grimace, as if tasting sour milk, they spat out, "I don't want to live to 100!"

There it was. . .that was my problem to solve. That is the change I want to inspire in the world. I will change the culture of aging. On many levels, the Baby Boomer generation, of which I am part, *can* change their outlook on aging. We *can* redefine *old;* we *can* set the example for the generations that follow; we *can* show them that getting *older* is not just getting **old**—it's not finished, out of date, useless, non-functioning; we *can* live that way as an example; we *can* embrace the possibilities that life after 60 offers every one of us.

2020 sounded an alarm for Baby Boomers. As many were just beginning their retirements or on the verge of retiring the way they planned and saved and dreamed, the world stopped, doors closed, fear set in, masks and hazmat suits were donned, and we receded, retreated, and shut down for a long restless nap.

I was one of them. I was fortunate to work in a business (real estate) that was considered essential. It meant, except for a couple of months, I was able to work and earn a living. At home, my husband was not as fortunate. As a dentist with an autoimmune disease, over 70 and on immunosuppressants, he was unable to continue to work while the virus raged. We learned over the next two-plus years a new rhythm, to balance our personal economy, to socialize and connect in new ways while staying healthy.

During that time, I moved from journaling to writing. I joined a networking group that meets on Zoom, and I started meeting entrepreneurs of all ages and levels with whom I interact every week. I started other networking groups with different people who share and brainstorm and vent regularly. I started a weekly family zoom call that has brought my siblings and me closer and more in touch than we have ever been.

I'm a published author! I'm a writer. It's hard for me to say that. I never thought of myself as a writer before, but I always enjoyed writing. I just didn't think I was worthy of being called a writer. Today, I am. That's the product of a mindset shift. Shifting into "inner gear" gives me confidence. I'm driving now. I have a lot to say.

I'm building a platform. Whenever I say that people look a little confused, some will sheepishly squeak, "What's a platform?" Most will give me that look that says, *how nice.*

My platform is called Graceing Agefully™. I'm sharing my experience of life after 60 with whoever is willing to read or listen. I want fellow Baby Boomers to share their experiences, wins, and losses. I think history will remember us as "Baby Bloomers" in the second half of life.

I have a dream—one day young people will see aging as something to look forward to. They will honor the elders of the community and aspire to build meaning into their lives. They will see growing old as *growing.* They will see opportunities and possibilities ahead at every age. They will be surrounded by examples of centenarians who continue to push the limits and make contributions to society.

For you, dear reader, I hope what you find in this chapter and Graceing Agefully will be a tiny spark that lights your flame in the second half.

THE PRACTICE

DO ONE THING EVERY DAY THAT SCARES YOU!

When the opportunity was presented to write a chapter in a compilation book about mindset, I was all in, *Hell yes!* I knew that mindset was the most important first step in Graceing Agefully or just living your best life in the second half. I signed up right away. I knew I had something to say, I just didn't know exactly what it was. Part of that problem is that **mindset is everything!** It is also no-thing. Try writing about that!

Then, there's the word **mastery.** Yikes, that sounds so "I've figured it all out." Have I mastered the mindset? Hmm, not exactly.

Mindset is a practice. Mindset is a muscle. Mindset is temporal. It's not intellectual, and despite the word implying its location, it's not *in* the mind. The mind can exercise a powerful influence over it, as can the physical body, spirit, external energy, dreams, and even what you eat. I couldn't even find a definition in Webster's dictionary for mindset. It's one of those words we hear every day, we feel we know what it means, but it's nearly impossible to define or describe.

With that disclaimer, I'm going to share a practice that's helping me get stronger and more confident living "inside out."

I have a card on my vision board that says, "Do one thing every day that scares you." It's attributed to Eleanor Roosevelt. When I first put that card on my vision board, it had a weightier meaning in my mind. I thought it had to be something big and really scary—jumping out of an airplane big. As I stared it down, over time, I realized that I resist *a lot* out of fear. I resist things I'm reluctant to admit because I think they seem trivial to someone else.

The practice of doing one thing every day that scares you starts with understanding what scares you. I've defined what scares me as the things I resist. I resist discomfort.

For example, I don't like confrontation or conflict, do you? I tend to go quiet when I disagree with someone. It goes back to the voice I suppressed for the first half of my life. I never spoke up; I didn't want to hurt anyone's feelings. Speaking up as a lone voice in a crowded room of opponents is very scary. It's also a mindset muscle builder.

I recommend starting with what you resist. Maybe you resist making a phone call; you know the one you say you're going to make every day to reconnect, heal a relationship, apologize, ask for help, maybe ask about a job?

Maybe you've been planning to start exercising, but you're not ready. The hardest part is taking the first step. It's also the most rewarding. Start small, but achievable. Do it every day, non-negotiable. One pushup. One deep knee bend. Walk for five minutes. Sounds silly, but either you commit to one and do ten or realize, even one is not easy, but you can do it. Every time you take action and do one thing, you build confidence. Remember, the hardest one is the first one. Once you do it on day one, you check the box. You did it!

I have a list of my MDRs (Minimum Daily Requirements). It's an assortment of things that add up to "done" every day. On the days when "I don't have time" to exercise, my MDR is 20 minutes of walking or Peloton. Since it is my MDR, I fit it in. It may not be my goal activity level for the week, but it is my goal for the day. On the days "I don't have time," I fit it in; it's also **non-negotiable.** That does more for my mindset in 20 minutes than a one-hour class. I have more confidence and feel strong because I'm done for the day even though I didn't have time!

In the second half of life, we can get stronger day by day. Life doesn't happen overnight; it's cumulative. Muscles aren't built and strong overnight. They're gradually, systematically built by consistent work, consistently gradually increasing weight. We're building mindset muscles in the second half by facing our discomfort head-on.

Doing one thing that scares you every day is like resistance training to build a healthy, confident, growth mindset.

Jennifer Sproul is in her late 60s, a *Baby Bloomer*, and the founder of the platform Graceing Agefully.

"The youngest Baby Boomers are over 60 now and the centenarian (100 years+) population is one of the fastest growing segments of our population. When I asked some of my fellow Boomers what they would do differently if they *knew* they would live to 100, the answer was a resounding, "I don't want to live to 100!"That's why I built Graceing Agefully."

The mission of Graceing Agefully is to change the culture of aging, to help others increase their health span, not just their lifespan.

"I understand why they feel this way; examples of the elderly in our culture today are dominated by images of chronic illness, disability, loneliness, dependency and pain, and even poverty rendered by a system of care that costs more than the majority of the population can afford. Who would look forward to that? I am only halfway to the end, so I've focused on the opportunity ahead, not focusing on what will be lost in the years ahead. This is a time to learn, grow and prosper; I am creating a well-integrated life in my second half. Graceing Agefully is my platform to share the experiences I'm having, the books that inspire me, the podcasts that teach me, and the stories of others who are living well-integrated lives and staying healthy into their 80s, 90,s and 100s."

Jennifer is a realtor with Washington Fine Properties in the Washington, DC, metropolitan area. She lives with her husband Raymond, a dentist, and their two cats, Sam and Jack.

Connect with Jennifer:

GraceingAgefully platform access: www.graceingagefully.com
GraceingAgefully FacebookGroup:
https://www.facebook.com/groups/326259166129920

Jennifer Sproul, Realtor website: www.jennifersproul.com

Email: jennifer.sproul@wfp.com

Mobile phone: 240-888-9495

"After my epiphany that I could live to 120 and was only halfway, I started surveying people, many of whom were in their 70s. I asked them 'What if you learned from an unimpeachable source that you will live to be at least 100, what would you do differently?' Without exception, the responses were quick and decisive. With a grimace, as if tasting sour milk, they spat out 'I don't want to live to 100!' There it was...that was my problem to solve, that is the change I want to inspire in the world."

~ Jennifer Sproul

Chapter 20

MANIFEST YOUR WILDEST DREAMS

A LIFE-CHANGING MEDITATION PRACTICE

Lori Pieper, Total Well-Being Coach, Meditation Instructor

MY STORY

You have to stop!

Did you hear me?

If you don't stop now, don't blame me!

That was my soul screaming at me as I sat down at my computer that morning. I will remember that day forever as the day I had my first, but unfortunately not my last, panic attack because of work.

On this particular day, I felt I had lost my very soul to "the man"—Corporate America. This feeling would remain with me for quite some time until I finally learned that self-*care* is not self*ish*. Actually, it's quite the opposite.

I lived through tragic events in the past without panicking. I was in New York and watched the World Trade Center towers fall on 9/11. We could see it clearly from our office windows. And yes, my heart ached and

I cried many tears, having witnessed such callous barbarism. Yet, I still had hope in my soul for a brighter future.

However, on this bleak Monday, I felt trapped with no way out, and with no one to turn to.

I now know that our worst days can become the impetus for unbelievably positive transformations. It's like the ugly duckling becoming the white swan. I believe these struggles are life giving us opportunities to rise above and become our best selves. And even though I haven't attained white swan status yet, here is one ugly duckling transformation story.

MELTDOWN MONDAY

"Beep, beep, beeeeeep," the alarm clock blared.

Ugh, I thought as I reached my arm out of the warm respite of my covers to turn off the alarm.

I usually hit the snooze once or twice, but this morning I just turned the damn thing off. The sheets softly caressed my body while my pillow cradled my head like the comfort of a mother's lap.

The world will have to survive without me today, I thought as I rolled over and pulled the covers over my head.

But, what about your clients, Lori? My ego-brain asked.

I don't care. Go away!

But, Lori, they need you. My ego-brain knew how to trick me into caring, but it didn't work this time.

Nice try, but it's not working today.

What will people think, Lori? That you're lazy? That you suck at your job?

Shit! My ego-brain played the "What will people think?" card and with that, my quiet "safe space" was no longer safe.

Dammit! Can't sleep now. May as well get up and get to work. But I refuse to shower, so there! I thought in total defiance, as if anyone cared. After all, I worked from home.

With eyes still half-closed, I swung my feet out from under the warm covers, put on my slippers and sweats, trudged out to the kitchen and made coffee and toast. The smell of the coffee brewing and the bread toasting did offer some solace as I trudged to my home office and turned on my computer.

As I waited for my computer to boot, I doctored my coffee with cream and stevia, generously buttered my toast, and still bleary eyed, I sat down at my desk.

I held the cup of coffee in both hands, feeling its comforting warmth. Inhaling the chocolate raspberry aroma, I took a few sips and then took a bite of my toast. I was feeling almost human.

And then it happened. I was faced with the login screen. I knew what was awaiting me once I signed in: At least one hundred *new* emails adding to the existing 1,000 unread. Yes, I'm being serious, and that's on a slow day. I suddenly felt like I was at war. A war I could never win.

I couldn't touch my keyboard. It was as if there were 1,000 snakes slithering all over it.

How would you feel about placing your hands anywhere near that? Think about it. The feeling of your skin crawling? The utter gross-outed-ness? Yeah, I made up that word, but you know what I mean.

That was how I felt about my keyboard that day. I seriously couldn't put my hands anywhere near it. My stomach was no longer tolerating the toast and coffee. Things that gave me pleasure just moments ago, were curdling in my stomach. Yes, I was at war, fighting for my very soul.

Lori, your customers are counting on you, said the task-master ego-brain.

Please, I can't do this today, said the timid child inside me that wanted to run and hide.

You're getting paid good money to do your job, now do it, you big baby!

But, I don't wanna. I pleaded like a pouty child.

And then it happened. My stomach was in knots. My hands started to shake. My throat tightened to the point I was having difficulty breathing. Tears were welling up in my eyes. And then the dam broke.

The emotions I suppressed deep inside for years, ignoring the desperate cries for help from my body and soul, began to bubble up screaming, "You will no longer ignore us!"

I don't know the definition of a panic attack versus an anxiety attack. Nor do I know if what I experienced that day was either one. What I do know is I was unable to ignore my body and soul any longer. They were telling me: It's time to focus on you before you're lost forever.

I sat at my desk and cried like a baby with colic for at least an hour. If you've ever been around a baby with colic, you know what I mean. Somehow, through the tears, I emailed my boss to say I was taking a mental health day. And then I cried some more.

Luckily, I had already been through yoga teacher training and knew several healing techniques to lift me out of my depths of despair—but just barely. I took the day to take care of myself, but I knew one day of pampering would *not* sustain me long term.

I had become so overworked and overwhelmed that I was ineffective at my job and my life. It's one thing to be ineffective at my job because of job-related stress, but how can I allow myself to be ineffective in my life because of work? That's insane. And yet, it was my reality. My guess is many of you reading this can relate.

Why do we put work and others' needs ahead of our own, even when our hearts and souls are screaming for a little TLC? That answer is different for everyone, but for me, it was because I was often paralyzed by the "what will people think" syndrome. It was instilled in me at a very young age and reinforced throughout my life.

My first memory of experiencing the "what will people think" syndrome occurred one spring afternoon. I was only five or six at that time. The flowers were in full bloom, filling the air with their sweet scent. The sky was a royal blue with beautiful fluffy white clouds. Mom and I were sitting on the front porch, as people did back then. Mom was reading the paper and I was coloring.

My neighbor was just getting home from work and as he got out of the car, he called out a friendly, "Hello."

We were good friends with our neighbors and pleasantries were exchanged. My neighbor held up a small American flag, like those you see lining the streets at Fourth of July parades.

"Lori, do you want this flag?" he asked.

"No thank you," I replied, continuing to color.

"Really, you can have it," he replied, knowing I was shy and might be intimidated.

"No, really. Thank you anyway."

My neighbor said, "Okay," put the flag on his lamppost and went inside.

"Lori, why didn't you take the flag?" Mom asked.

"Because I didn't want it."

"Well, you should have taken it anyway. You hurt his feelings. What will he think?"

Well, as you can imagine, I felt terrible that I hurt my neighbor's feelings. Actually, I have no idea if I really hurt his feelings, but my mom said I did, and I believed her.

I was just being honest. And now I felt terrible and I wondered if he would hate me forever.

Every day for what seemed like years, I saw that flag on my neighbor's lamppost and it reminded me of how I allegedly hurt his feelings, and I wondered what he thought of me. That's a lot for a little kid. And that was the first brick in my "what will people think" prison.

Back to meltdown Monday. As I was doing my self-healing work, I had a vision from my early twenties. It was a friend of mine saying, "Lori, I saw you in your car the other day. I beeped and waved, but you didn't see me. I could tell you were into your music. You were singing and jamming and smiling. Damn, girl, you're always smiling!"

Wow! That thought hit me hard. I remembered those days in my Camaro with the windows down on a sunny day. I could feel the wind in my hair as I drove and danced in my seat. The radio would be blasting and I'd be so into my music I didn't care what people thought. The freedom I felt was powerful.

I seemed to have forgotten how to enjoy just singing in my car, or dancing around my house with the music blaring. I forgot how to be happy just being me. I felt my heart sink as I asked myself: *What the hell happened to me?*

The answer is I became so immersed in work that I stopped realizing the harm it was doing to my mind, body, and soul. Overwork and stress make us old, cranky, and sick! It's true! But that's for another book.

Soon after Meltdown Monday, I attended a Chopra event and I learned Primordial Sound Mantra (PSM) Meditation. Prior to that, I tried other forms of meditation, but believed I could never meditate because my brain just wouldn't stop thinking. I couldn't "clear my mind," so I stopped trying.

But the PSM meditation instruction busted the many myths that held me back, and I quickly established a regular meditation practice.

The changes in my life were truly magical. Solutions to life's problems my brain could never have imagined were coming to me out of nowhere. Meditation helped me manifest my perfect job, my dream home, and the perfect transition from "workin' for the man" to being the entrepreneur and author I am today.

More importantly, it was the daily benefits of meditation that made an impact. People at work and home noticed that I was more compassionate and laid back and laughed more. I was feeling more alive than I had in a long time.

But my job was still over-the-top stressful. I wanted a job that was a lot less intense. I looked at the job postings regularly to no avail. So, I began setting an intention before each meditation, as follows: "I want to stay with the same company. I want a job that is a lot less stressful and pays a similar salary."

After several weeks of using this intention, one morning as I meditated, a voice rippled up from within and said, *I am a teacher.* Even though there was no sound, I heard it clearly. I knew it came from my heart.

I finished my meditation, got ready for work, sat down at my computer and within an hour, a friend from the corporate office called me.

"Hey, Lori, it's Mike!" he said.

"To what do I owe this honor?"

"I have an opening in the education department. We need an instructor."

My heart leaped!

Is this real? I asked myself.

Did God really just give me a heads-up during my meditation?

Uh, yep, I think so.

How cool is that?

Before this, it never occurred to me to reach out to Mike, or review his job postings. I was so into my own misery, my brain couldn't imagine being an instructor as a viable option. Meanwhile, in meditation, the Universe saw all possibilities and truly found the perfect job for me, where I was able to flourish.

I applied for the job and within a month I started my new position, at the same company, with less stress, and a similar income. In my eyes this was a miracle.

Miracles do happen and you can manifest yours!

THE PRACTICE

Deepak Chopra, M.D., when asked the difference between prayer and meditation, once responded, "Prayer is talking to God. Meditation is listening to God."

In this practice, your intention is your prayer. It states your desire. Meditation is going inward to that place of silence where you listen to God.

I use the words God and Universe somewhat interchangeably. Growing up, my image of God was a white man with a white beard sitting on a cloud looking down on us. And like Santa Claus, God's noting who's naughty or nice. After many years of digging deeper into spirituality, I often choose to use *Universe* because, for me, it expands my old limited view of God—and God has no limits. I now know God/Universe as a presence and power all around us, guiding us toward our dreams. When we close ourselves off with stress, worry, and anger, we can't hear the sacred wisdom or recognize the synchronicities of God's guidance.

That's just my view.

Back to meditation.

Meditation trains your brain not to *attach* to your thoughts. However... **You will have thoughts!**

I wanted that to stand out because it's the number one reason why people feel they can't meditate. You cannot stop your thoughts, so don't even try to *clear your mind.* The more you try to stop your thoughts the more they will persist.

The goal is *not to attach* to those thoughts. What do I mean by that? Let's say you hear a motorcycle as you're meditating, and you start thinking of the places you could go if you had a motorcycle, or what type of motorcycle you would buy, etc. That's *attaching* to that thought. If instead you hear a motorcycle and simply go back to your predetermined point of focus, then you're meditating.

In this practice, our predetermined point of focus will be repeating a word or phrase, called a mantra.

Meditation is a *practice*. With practice, your thoughts will become less and less distracting. Since we have 80-90 thousand thoughts a day and 80% are negative, as you detach from your thoughts, you will find you experience less negativity and more joy and calm.

Without those thoughts distracting you, you'll begin to get clarity from your heart. Your heart and soul laugh for no reason and love fully and completely. Sounds pretty good, huh?

As for manifesting your dreams, setting an intention is key. This tells God/Universe what you want. Yes, God already knows, but if *you* aren't clear about what you want, you won't recognize the synchronicities showing you the path to your dreams.

You want to make your intention clear and positive. For example, if you want to have a better relationship with your spouse you might be inclined to say, "Please stop us from fighting all the time!" However, here you're focusing on what you *don't* want. When setting your intention, turn it around and say what you *do* want, like, "Please allow my spouse and me to be kind to each other even when we disagree."

Ask for what you *do* want, not what you *don't* want.

THE MEDITATION

Below is a short meditation practice. The amount of time you spend meditating is up to you. I suggest you start with five minutes a day and every one to two weeks, add five minutes to build up to 20 minutes, twice a day.

When you first wake up, and between work and your evening meal are the two recommended times of day to meditate. But, it's more important *to meditate!* Do what works for your schedule.

- Find a comfortable seated position. This can be in a chair, or on the floor with your legs crossed.

- Set a timer. You likely have one on your phone. Set the ending bell to be something calming, not jarring.

- Close your eyes.
- Inhale slowly through your nose, expanding your belly. Expanding your belly when you inhale signals your nervous system that all is well, triggering relaxation.
- Exhale through the mouth with a sigh.
- Repeat the above two to three times.
- Keeping your eyes closed, breathe normally. Be mindful to expand your belly on the inhale.
- Set your intention. Remember to be clear and positive. Once you set the intention, let it go. Trust the Universe to work its magic.
- Silently repeat this mantra to yourself: OM SHRIM NAMAHA.
- This is pronounced:
  - OM – like 'HOME' without the 'H.'
  - SHRIM – shreem
  - NAMAHA – like the Yamaha motorcycle, but starting with 'N' not 'Y.'

The mantra loosely means bringing abundance back to yourself. I mention this so you can feel comfortable with the mantra. Please stay focused on repeating the mantra, not on its meaning. Trust the Universe will bring you what you need as you do the work.

Commit to the time you set for your meditation no matter how many thoughts you have. The barrage of thoughts are releasing stress and that is good. As you get distracted, gently bring your attention back to the mantra.

Don't judge or badger yourself if you feel you aren't "doing it right." *You are doing it right.* Struggling puts you back into fight-or-flight mode which has the opposite effect of meditation.

FINAL THOUGHT

You got this. Trust that you are "doing it right." Be consistent, and welcome the ensuing magic. You deserve it!

For recorded meditations, FAQs, and options for going deeper, please visit my website:

https://www.JourneyToInnerJoy.com/resources

Lori Pieper is the founder of Journey to Inner Joy, LLC. She's a certified Chopra Total Well-being Coach, Chopra PSM Meditation instructor, Reiki Master, yoga instructor, and Chopra Perfect Health: Ayurvedic Lifestyle instructor. Lori brings the magic of a unique blend of healing practices and life-changing wisdom to you through Total Well-being coaching.

Her mission is to help women who feel they have lost their soul "workin'" for the man," aka, Corporate America. She helps these amazing ladies to reclaim their lives and know that self-care is not selfish. When you feel healthy and strong, you are better able to lift yourself and others up.

Lori's personal journey to clarity was beautiful, necessary, and worth it—and expertly prepared her to understand and serve her clients. As a coach, she uses her training and deep intuition to assist her clients on their journey. She listens with compassion as she guides them through soul-searching practices, giving them the clarity to make decisions that are right for them.

"Do I change careers?" "Do I start my own business?" Scary questions like these become easier when the answer comes from the heart and soul. The brain and ego will often give fear-based answers keeping you from making the brave choices needed for your well-being.

Lori's clients gain the courage to set boundaries at work and at home in order to honor their own well-being. They gain the clarity to know what is and is not negotiable. These amazing ladies learn to be fully alive and realize they are happy for no damn reason!

This is your life. It's time to live it with clarity, choice, and passion.

Connect with Lori:

Website: https://www.journeytoinnerjoy.com/

LinkedIn: https://www.linkedin.com/in/loripieper/

Facebook: https://www.facebook.com/JourneyToInnerJoy

Instagram: https://www.instagram.com/loripieper23/

Email: Lori@JourneyToInnerJoy.com

To book a free consultation:

https://www.reikihealingnetwork.com/loripieper/well-being-consultation

"Stop. Be silent. It is in this silence you can hear your truth bubbling up from your heart. Your heart's wisdom guides you to live your truth, not someone else's. Only then can you be truly successful."

~ Lori Pieper

Chapter 21

AWARENESS GIVES YOU A CHOICE

CHOOSE LOVE EVERY DAY

Laura Di Franco

I know meeting the experts in this book has inspired you. I love that. That's part of the mission of this book and my company. Reading stories of people just like you should help you understand what's possible. We hope you're sitting there with a light bulb moment about just what kind of life is waiting for you.

You can read books, learn tools, and feel inspired. You can hear words from a friend, mentor, or inspirational speaker and feel those goosebumps. You might get a download about the next best steps. All of these moments are amazing. It's what you do with them, the action you take, that's the catalyst for the change.

You will not feel clear, confident, or courageous first. You must act *with* the purpose-driven fears. You must take action *with* the feelings you have inside. When you're on the other side of that fear, the clarity, confidence, and courage will show up. If you wait to feel that way before you leap, you'll be waiting a long time, probably frozen.

With awareness, you get a choice. Making an aligned choice and taking action is the change. I hope you'll take some action after reading this book. I hope you'll choose love more often, especially the kind you shower on yourself. Choose a chapter to experience today. Carve out some time to read and practice the author's tool. Protect that time and take action. If you have a question or need some guidance, be brave and reach out to the author of the chapter.

These books are a starting point. They're meant to give you a powerful toolkit. They're also created to give you a powerful healing community to immerse yourself in, reach out to, and get help from. You don't have to do this alone. You're not meant to.

There's healing as you read these words. There's healing as you practice the tools. There's more healing as you embark upon the inner work on your own. And there's even more healing when you have a coach or mentor to guide you. Healing also happens within your community when you find a safe space to be your full-on self. What I hope you'll adopt as a regular question on this journey is: What else is possible? On the most difficult days, I hope you'll take that deep, pelvic bowl breath, pause, and ask yourself that important question. And then open yourself up to love.

If you're feeling moved by what one of our authors wrote, and are inspired, reach out to them. You can also join the author experts from many of our world-changing books, including this one, in The Brave Healer Book Club on Facebook. Be brave. Take some action as you close this book. Maybe there's something you haven't learned yet that could change everything!

The Most Important Thing
By Laura Di Franco

The most important thing in my life?

Waking to love, in every possible way
that helps me feel fiercely alive.
My ability to take that inspiration,
available at any moment,
even the impossible ones.

Being awake enough to choose love,
no matter what,
no matter where,
no matter who,
no matter how difficult,

no matter how ripped-open it leaves me. . .
. . . this is the most important thing.

To look at another with complete acceptance,
understanding,
and compassion.
No matter what they've said
or what they've done.
To forgive and move into love
letting that energy be what
infiltrates my heart.

I always have a choice,
so I must attempt to choose love,
not out of duty or obligation
to my parents or teachers
but to my soul.
A promise to take radical, complete care of myself. . .
. . . the same self who'll then
and only then,
have the other-worldly capacity
to give what's necessary to make a change.

The most important thing in my life
is a wild, crazy, big-ass, unexplainable love,
an unfiltered, out-of-the-box, bigger version
than I was originally taught,
a flavor created by me,
tasted only by those who dare
and delighted in by those
courageous enough
to step into another level of vibration
without truly knowing what's in store,
willing to risk it all,
willing to come crashing down,
and rise back up,

dripping in the sacred bath of the full moon
and ready to take on the world.

The most important thing in my life
is the warrior love
I was born to be.

With Warrior Love,

Laura

BECOME A
BESTSELLING AUTHOR

Your words change the world when you're brave enough to share them. It's time to be brave.

Are you ready to become an author in one of our bestselling books? Or lead your own book project?

Reach out to speak to the Brave Healer Productions publishing team by emailing: support@LauraDiFranco.com

THE BRAVE HEALER WRITERS RETREAT

Join us in the powerful red rock vortexes of Sedona, Arizona, for The Brave Healer Writers Retreat, where you'll enjoy experiences crafted to inspire, transform, and educate the world-changing badass you are. Our focus is to help you share your brave words and work with the world in a bigger way.

https://lauradifranco.com/writersretreat/

You were born, so you're worthy. Your message matters.
What if the thing you're still a little afraid to share is
exactly what someone needs to hear to change
(or even save) their life? It's time to be brave.

www.ingramcontent.com/pod-product-compliance
Lightning Source LLC
Chambersburg PA
CBHW061144120626
46546CB00005B/1927